Eclectic
Neil Moffatt

The purpose of this book is to share and pass on some of the things that I have deeply enjoyed discovering and reading about in my life.

An eclectic mix, subject to occasional updates and additions.

Cover photograph by the author

Vector art copyright Curly Line Vectors :

https://www.vecteezy.com/free-vector/curly-line

https://www.vecteezy.com/free-vector/soccer by Vecteezy

Revision history

October 2019	First draft
November 2019	**Ageing** chapter added
October 2020	**Mental gravities** chapter added
July 2024	First chapter completely revised
May 2025	Some tweaks

Feedback would be most welcome

moffatt.neil@gmail.com

Contents

Understanding your mind

The relationship between the
conscious and the unconscious

It is said that the conscious mind is so small a part of our brain that it is like the tip of an iceberg, with the unconscious mind vast in size beneath the waves. But it is even more extreme than that.

The conscious mind is more like a snowball on that iceberg. It is tiny, yet it looms big and central to our lives. And we feel that it controls the unconscious – that it is the 'CEO' of the brain. But it really does not.

Much of what you believe about your mind will be unravelled in the coming pages. In a sense this will be a little scary, but should actually be an enlightening and lightening process. Life can be relentlessly intense and demanding, and being lighter of outlook will help greatly.

Focal to this story will necessarily be the relationship between the conscious mind and the unconscious mind. The conscious mind is often limited to just the power of veto – not so much free-will as free-wont.

However, this is less of a problem than it seems, so a good time to spell out its limitations.

It is patently clear that our internal bodily functions are autonomic. We are not consciously even aware of the behaviour of our internal organs, immune system, oxygen transport and so on. We can hear the heart beat, and mostly get notified of body illness or injury, but the conscious mind has no direct bearing on these matters. Our role is cursory or high level – limited to choosing or not to rest an injured hamstring for example. We do not partake in its repair.

Likewise, we have a high level of control – or directing role – in how our body moves. But again, the billions of cells involved in those movements are outside of awareness. We need not know nor direct at a detailed level. So we conceive how to hit the tennis ball, but rely on the unconscious mind to convert our desires into coordinated body movements to carry out our tennis strokes and all that exhausting movement chasing the ball around the court.

The conscious mind is clumsily slow, so if we try to take over some of the process, it will lose the efficiency and flow that is automated in our unconscious motor movement sequences.

This difference in capability is most clearly apparent when learning to drive a car – distracted one day by your driving instructor you realise that the unconscious mind has taken over. Much as it will later do when you finally notice that your deep train of thought has no awareness of having driven the last ten miles. We can be aware of driving the car, but the conscious mind is not doing the driving.

You can directly see how limited the conscious mind is by holding out your hands in front of you so that both are visible. But you will notice that you can only pay full attention to one of your hands at a time. Our conscious mind is single-threaded, only able to attend fully to one thing at a time. We can still multi-task, but only one task can have our conscious attention, the remainder will need to be automated by the unconscious. Like stirring food in a saucepan while thinking about your plans later in the day. We can only fully attend to multiple things by task-switching. We focus back and forth between two or more activities. And that also incurs a switching cost to one degree or other.

Much of each day, most of us are on a similar 'auto-pilot'. We are literally oblivious of what we are doing while pondering something 'more important' in our minds. We reply that we are fine when asked by a stranger we pass how we feel. But if we pause and reflect we realise that this is not true. Our automatic neutral response took over to save us effort.

Of course, the conscious mind is involved in big decision making, but considerably less so than we realise. Much of the fuel for decisions, and thinking in general, is supplied from memories and calculations by our unconscious mind. It percolates up in a way that feels like the conscious mind is the originator.

Since we can and often do automate decision making, we may find that we have stopped watching our TV programme to go to the toilet rather than wait until the commercial break. It happened quickly, automatically, reflexively. After we resume watching, we are puzzled why we had 'chosen' to do go to the toilet and thereby miss something crucial on the programme we were watching. Auto-pilot often does not serve us terribly well.

Evolution tends to always have sound reason for how things have evolved into their current state. So the conscious mind has to exist for a reason. Some things are left for it to decide rather than automate, but why the awareness that goes much deeper than permit high-level decision making? And quite what, why and where the demarcation line is between conscious and unconscious decision apportioning remains unclear from what I have read in many books on the mind.

The conscious mind has to be a focal decision making part of our brain, or why else would the unconscious go to such great lengths to flood it with emotions and feelings and thoughts? It receives increasingly urgent full bladder feelings in case we stick too long watching our 'precious' TV programme. And we can experience intense pain if we mobilise our injured hamstring too much.

The conscious mind also receives summary sensory data about the world from sight, hearing, touch and so on as informational fuel in our high level decision making.

It also receives thoughts (and even the words spoken in conversation) from the unconscious. Yet we really feel that the conscious mind is again the originator. Do we really not know what we will say until we have spoken it? Sadly, it mostly true. It is more that we consciously steer and prioritise what the unconscious wants us to say.

Likewise, our beliefs and views on life are deeply embedded in the unconscious.

In summary, the conscious mind has some roles in high level decision making, fuelled by perceptions, feelings, emotions, beliefs, morals, ethics, views and thoughts from the unconscious. The unconscious is like a summary place in the brain where all high level information coalesces.

Genetic forces

But there is a theme of unconscious influence in how the information is presented and prioritised. And behind this influence is the combination of our genetic inheritance, life experiences and the conclusions created from these experiences. To a large extent, we are a vehicle for our genes to propagate themselves. We are driven in two principle ways to that primary end – to survive and to reproduce.

Our lives are deeply bound to these two ways. They influence and infiltrate a vast amount of what we do.

At root, these principle drives of survival and reproduction do not care how happy we are, or how much we achieve, or who we are friends with and enemies to. These are factors that affect the drives, but they are not the primary focus of the drives.

If we were content and happy all the time we would likely jeopardise our survival prospects, much as happens when taking powerful drugs. So we are drip fed feelings of pleasure and happiness enough to ensure we are getting life done in order to survive and have and care for offspring.

This is pretty stark stuff. As you will see, what suits survival and reproduction often does not suit how we might want to live our lives. Especially as our genetics is way behind on the adaption curve to adjust to the rapid changes in human lives over the past few centuries. Which is why the desire for sugary food that was rare but safe in its rarity in the past gives us problems nowadays.

An observation I made some while back I feel illustrates how outdated our genetics has become. Pornographic images on paper or screen can arouse and entertain us. Our brain should not be aroused since there is no chance of sexual congress. It still presumes that the vision of an enticing semi-clad or naked body necessarily means we have a chance to copulate.

As a foundational matter, our unconscious mind, driven by genetics, has a heavy influence on how our lives pan out. The whole point in writing about all this is to show how valuable it is to temper that influence. We really should not heed outdated genetic instincts or urges. In general, we really should not always heed what our unconscious thrusts upon us.

To give clue to the relentless nature of the 'get life done' unconscious drives, you need only shut your eyes and observe the incessant stream of rumination, reflection and planning thoughts that bombards your conscious mind. A bombardment that will continue even when you really want to just sit calmly with a clear mind. Here you will see most clearly the force of our genetic heritage.

Energy conversation

There is an additional drive that I must now introduce. The brain is about 2% of the body mass yet consumes about 25% of body energy. This energy hungry nature has created a constant focus on preserving energy – an economy drive. This has an extraordinarily large influence on our minds, often in a necessarily compromising fashion, much as energy preservation when tired playing sport can lead to mistakes and bad technique.

But the impact of energy conservation on our minds is multi-faceted and deep.

Perceiving the world

I have now set the stage for more detailed explorations where the survival, reproduction and economising drives are a foundational triad.

Let's start with a simple expression of unconscious influence – one that you will experience most days. As you read these sentences, the shapes of the ink on paper are seen by the eyes and interpreted by the unconscious mind as words. It is actually very hard to look at a word and not automatically be made aware of its meaning. That meaning is attached to what we perceive.

Similarly, when we sniff a rose we experience the bouquet. But attached is a warm feeling – it is a pleasant experience to smell that rose. Our perceptions have 'flavours' of all kinds attached by the unconscious. Perception invariably has automatic judgements, thoughts and/or feelings attached.

When we hear the sound of a seagull squawking overhead it is not just a clean and simple perception of that sound, but judgements are often added. The sound can feel ugly, annoying, intrusive. It can remind us of our belief that these creatures are a kind of vermin. Listen with these judgements pushed into the background and the sound is actually often quite pretty.

In this simple example, you start to get a feel of how our unconscious manipulates and influences our lives.

Our bodies perceive a vast amount of sensory 'data', handled by unconscious mind and body working on concert. At the highest level, summary data is built and passed to the conscious mind as the unconscious mind sees fit. We must have this kind of executive summary since the conscious mind is slow and lumbering and has limited faculties. This summarisation also aligns well with the economy drive.

It is prudent to point out that sensory data flow is bidirectional. Signals are both sent to and received from the eyes, nose, skin, limbs etc. The economy drive has created a predictive perception system to minimise energy expenditure. The unconscious predicts how are arm will move and how our hand will grab as we start to reach out for our cup of coffee. As we move, the unconscious is generally only interested in any sensory data that shows a deviation from the predictions. Novel matters. When our fingers slip on the handle and the cup is knocked over, only then is sensory data fully received and acted upon.

A fundamentally curious and possibly disconcerting thing to understand is that all that our conscious experience of the world is actually a kind of hallucination or illusion. All that our senses receive is waves and/or particles – sound, sight, touch all arrive this way. After conversion to electrical impulses they are processed in the unconscious mind into a form that makes sense to the mind and body. These forms are proxies for the real world. The bright red flower we see is a mental construct. The colour red does not exist out there in the real world. We perceive only light waves reflected off the flower that do not have the wavelength of 'red' light. We do not even see the flower but only perceive light waves bounding off it.

Sound likewise is constructed from the electrical signals that summarise the air waves that impinge on our ear drums. There is no sound out there since sound is only a product or function of perception. Our unconscious creates all those rich sounds of an orchestra in full pomp and glory.

This is a tricky concept to grasp. It is understandable if you reject this concept.

When we have an injury or illness, we will tend to feel pain. We may believe the pain resides in our injured hamstring, but the unconscious mind just fools the conscious mind into assigning it there – all pain is created by the unconscious. It too is a construct. The role of the pain is fortunately a good one – to protect us from aggravating a site of injury, or to rest when we have an illness. The pain generated by the unconscious is described as a *biopsychosocial* matter. Pain level is the result of a multi-factorial calculation! The unconscious takes into account our sensitivity, history, previous traumas, current emotional state and social situation. The 'reasoning' behind this is to generate the right amount of pain to protect the injury site. It is surprisingly not very well correlated with the actual level and nature of injury, especially as time passes. The unconscious can economise and stop checking the injury site but instead just reflexively generate pain when the injury site is mobilised. For conditions such as frozen shoulder, it can continue to protect long after the original injury has healed (which generally takes at most six months). The survival instinct errs on the side of protection.

Perception of social matters can add layers of complexity. At root of our relationships with others is that survival drive – we will tend to favour self when we can, whilst also protecting our social status. And the economy drive means we can be lazy seeing and understanding others by presuming they are by default like us, and therefore we presume they should behave like us, have similar morals, ethics and beliefs. These biases make the already difficult social 'dances' we engage in even more prone to problems and misunderstandings. We seek to avoid damaging relationships or being ostracised for saying and doing socially bad things.

Beliefs and thoughts

We also perceive our internal world – the parts of what the unconscious mind channels to the conscious mind that go beyond matters of external world perception. I refer to all that mental chatter pervading every moment of our lives. Ruminations, beliefs, ideas, plans, thoughts, day dreams and so on. And much of this stream is tainted by distortions and biases and appended by feelings and emotions.

Regardless of the level of our ego, the survival instinct tended to place ourselves at the centre of our lives, and anything that might compromise our survival became a candidate to be downplayed or outright avoided. As a consequence, our genetics drives us to place the welfare of ourself, family and friends ahead of truth, honesty and rationality.

Really.

Beliefs become embedded and immune from reasoned argument. We see the morals and ethics that we have adopted as superior to those of others. Most people believe they are better than average drivers, more caring than others, more thoughtful.

A particularly egocentric behaviour is to attribute failings in others to their behaviour and decisions taken, but to see circumstances beyond our control for our own failings.

When we are angered and lose our temper, the unconscious mind hyper focuses on our point of view, aggressively promoting it whilst simultaneously blocking considerations of the opposing view of the person we are angered by. It can feel so natural to go with that temper. But we have, to an extent, lost our minds – lost the ability to be rational and reasonable.

Equally egocentrically, we treat matters close to home and self as more important than much more serious matters elsewhere. We dismiss quite readily what is remote in place and time from where and when we are. Even matters close to home we can sometimes dismiss – what ails someone is too readily glossed over if we have not experienced it ourselves.

And then there is the vast matter of our cognitive biases. Over 200 of them. These are mostly the consequence of a self-centred economically conceived view of life. A very prevalent one in these days of online social media is confirmation bias, where we read about matters that confirm our viewpoints and avoid matters and people that challenge them. We can also be prone to false consensus bias where we presume that most people will agree with our point of view. Politicians are extremely prone to this.

Pleasure, pain and seeking

I have already mentioned feelings that coerce us to rest an injury or go to toilet when our bladder is almost full. But there are more vital feelings that drive our lives. They have been there for millions of years in our ancestors and animals.

Further back, their roots lie in the early single cell creatures.

Approaching good things
Withdrawing from bad things

Single celled creatures seek out and approach food and avoid predators and other dangers. Our version of these most basic drives manifest as feelings. We are given doses of pleasure when we acquire food and sex and shelter and success in life. And we are given pain or ill feelings when we get into danger or injured or find bad food or engage in risky sexual encounters.

Pleasure and pain.

Push and pull.

But there is an additional motivational force. To seek. To explore. To get ahead in life. To achieve status. To get married. To get a fabulous new TV. A new home. To get married.

The hormone dopamine drives this seeking. And the unconscious wants us to keep seeking no matter what we already have. So here we find another perverting effect of the genetic drive to survive – it ramps up the seeking of new as it maximised the survival chances of our ancestors. Survival is largely predicated on the ability to adapt. So expanding into new domains and experiences increases our flexibility to adapt.

The unconscious is focussed on relatives – getting more, advancing in life – more than the absolutes of where we have gotten to so far. It is much like the novelty receptive nature of perceptions.
Downsides of that focus on more, more, more are of course many-fold. It explains why businesses tend to keep expanding. Why politicians keep wanting to grow the economy. Why the novelty of a new TV soon fades. Even when we get a pay rise we will feel disappointed if it is smaller than the rise of a colleague.

Relativity blinds us to the absolute again.

In my retirement and dotage, I have become enthralled and obsessed by arts and crafts. I have been trying all sorts of crafts I never attempted before. That I have more crafts to do in my house than I have time to do even in retirement still does not stop me being excited by the prospect of another new craft I discover and order. Doing so, my unconscious conveniently forgets to remind me that the novelty can and will fade fast. Fortunately, I do periodically return to and enjoy each craft.

A key feature of the dopamine seeking drive is that it disengages when what it seeks has been achieved. Then you become reliant on the pleasure that the new novelty supplies. And of course pleasure is short lived so that we are coerced to live on a hedonic treadmill, seeking new repeatedly. Each meal we eat looms large and tasty in anticipation, and before very long it is consumed and we are pretty much back to square one, albeit after a short period of satiety. A more subtle feature of the dopamine drive is how it tends to focus our minds on the plus side of what we seek. But when we get that new IKEA furniture kit home, we realise with sinking heart that assembly will be a nightmare ...

However, we can actually take advantage of dopamine by recognising that it gives us a nice low level trickle of anticipatory pleasure. Subtle but tangible pleasure as we look forward to a new book arriving through the post, to a long awaited meet-up with an old friend, to a new programme on TV. One person I spoke with a while back said that he arranged holidays far ahead in time simply to enjoy a longer period of warm anticipation.

Sadly, smartphones exploit the dopamine mechanism for commercial gain. Each new message creates a little dose of anticipatory dopamine. This in itself is not a problem. But it can become addictive. Very addictive. The average smartphone use is purportedly about five hours a day. Repeating the habit of checking our phones for the next dopamine kicks can create an impatience in our nature. It can weaken our attentional focus and duration of focus.

Multi-mind

Let us return to the conscious mind. It is what we see as part and parcel of our personality. We feel with great certainty that there is a stability and continuity of our personality, albeit with some evolution over the years since we are certainly now more mature and wiser than when young.

But this is an illusion. And to explain why, I introduce another concept that is rarely known or spoke about. We have a multi-mind, better known as a modular mind, that has some sound scientific vindication and validation.

There are a few chilling examples recorded of multiple personality disorder where a person switches between radically different personas. Their introversion, nature, voice and even bodily functions can change. They are unaware that they have switched as each personality is separate and complete.

The modular mind concept is very different from this. The very structure of the cerebral cortex is essentially a vast mass of tall neuronal circuits stacked like sardines. Each is generalised in purpose and they serve many disparate high level brain functions. For our purposes, we are interested in the modules that communicate with the conscious mind. The culprits for all that mental chatter, along with feelings, emotions and moods.

At each moment of the day, a few modules will be vying for conscious attention. The active ones will have most often been triggered or sustained by what we do. A great friend in my road here in Cardiff is like a local version of Michael Cain. Similar of age and as bluntly confrontational of nature, yet also a very loyal friend and warm at heart. A recent conversation with him moved from initial robust jollities into a more serious tone when I talked about news of atrocities in Palestine I saw on AlJazeera news on TV. The change of tone and thought in his voice was palpable. It was still the same person but conversation was markedly changed.

What happened here was that the mention of AlJazeera gave the green light for the AlJazeera mind modules to come to the fore.

Was his personality changed? Was this now his real personality?

The salient point here is that awareness/consciousness/personality are hot stepping from one suite of mind modules to the next throughout the day. There is no fixed nature of personality.

Those who claim, as I do, that they are sensitive creatures are both right and wrong. They are correct when the sensitive modules are in the forefront of our unconscious mind communication with the conscious mind, or when they are readily triggered into life by what is in focus. But when we have been treated unjustly, our revenge-seeking module will oust sensitive modules.

It is hard to overstate the importance of these matters. The conscious mind is taken on a merry dance throughout each day, as modules wheel in and out of awareness and influence. And many modules do wield influence, deploying strong emotions and feelings in concert with thoughts and decisions and beliefs presented to an often unwitting conscious awareness.

Unfortunately, these modules can be limited in scope – 'small minded' in fact. Such as the losing-one's-temper module. They have some interactions with other modules, but often sideline what was central to our attention just moments before. So we jump from one niche-perspective of the world and our view of it to the next.

When you stub your toe, the 'wow-that-really-hurt' module jumps right in and all other matters – modules – are thrust away. We can worry about a scary looking lump on our arm for days. It can consume our every thought – the 'get-this-sorted-soon' module endlessly nagging. When we hear to our delight that it is benign, we can relax and feel relieved. Except that the next problem in our lives that we must deal with – another module – rapidly reappears in the foreground. A problem that we had completely forgotten about that was in the shadow of that bigger matter is now back.

There is an extremely common problem in conversations between two people which I will illustrate with probably the most common type of scenario. Person A mentions how their knee has been giving them lots of problems. This triggers the unconscious in person B to wheel in the module that talks with others about their own recent leg pain. So they respond by talking about their problem. The module listening to person A was jostled to one side. What was needed was for person B's conscious mind to observe the urge to compare injuries and instead realise that first they must ask further about person A's injury. (This is being mindful – a topic to be covered shortly). This is an extraordinarily common conversational problem.

Likewise, when someone is being nice to us, the module glowingly happy to receive the positive attention pushes to one side the module that was attending to the life of the other person. So we often forget to reciprocate. This too is extremely common – one factor in life taking the limelight and putting other matters in the shade. You get the pattern now.

These rather simple modules are also prone to being primed. Behind our backs as it were – beneath conscious awareness. Propaganda involving repeated messages – lies even – primes and influences beliefs and judgements in modules.

Meditation

But there are well established antidotes and workarounds for these and other unconscious shortcomings. As with much that I have written about, Buddhism has supplied the practical techniques and methods for millennia. These seeped into Western culture in the last century or so, and are even taught in some schools to great effect.

I refer of course to Meditation and Mindfulness, but also to Acceptance, non-

Judgement, Equanimity and the thorny matter of Attachments.

I start with meditation as it is a core awareness training that enables the other faculties to manifest well.

The unconscious mind works on a probabilistic basis – it bombards the conscious mind enough to maximise the likelihood that it will respond appropriately – to 'get life done'. Or take a step towards reproduction. But it rarely gives us a break. And it rarely stops 'nagging' even when we have chosen and embarked on a response to its nags. Meditation is a method employed to give us a break from this endless onslaught.

The immediate effect is to calm both mind and body. Adrenaline and cortisol that help us drive our lives can ease back, allowing the parasympathetic nervous system to ramp up and start healing the body. Repeated meditative practice brings these same responses into our lives more readily even at the times when we are not meditating – it has a propagating effect.

Meditating is essentially the act of sustaining focussed attention. On something. Anything. It really does not have to be your breath while you sit crossed legged in the floor. I personally find that observing my breath affects my breathing. Better, I find, to focus attention on something, like a flower, or the flame of a candle for example, that is not affected by my attention. One of my favourite micro-meditations is watching the bubbles in my cup of tea swirl around and occasionally pop or merge. Another is simply to look at the aged skin in the backs of my hands. Doing such a thing makes us realise how little we do observe in the world. Meditating on a tree whilst sat in the park shows the tree in its full glory, and you start to merge with the tree. This may sound touchy-feely but try it for yourself to experience how relaxing it can be.

The calming effect is nice and also healthy but not the principle purpose. Instead, meditation trains us to be able to choose what we attend to, and what not to attend to. As you would guess by now, many matters thrust upon us by the unconscious are of poor or outdated value, so being aware enough to choose is pretty vital.

Even a few minutes a day can reap benefits. Better still, try to find 15 or 30 minute meditation slots each day.

At first, the bombardment of thoughts and feelings will overwhelm. Each time you try to focus on something a thought will distract you. If that happens, just observe the interruption. Surprisingly, doing this is still a form of meditating – of starting to observe and control your attention. (Using your phone much less will also really help). Eventually, you will be able to sustain focus for longer periods, even if the chatter sooner or later intervenes.

I personally find that micro-meditations on my walks are an easy and effective way of building up attention span. The first flower I stop to look at holds my attention loosely. The second I can look at with less effort. And before I walk to the third I generally find I have slowed my pace – in order to observe my footsteps. Now they are the subject of my meditation. The sustained focus starts to make me more sensitive to what I perceive. Compare with obsessive phone users who would admit to be terribly bored sat phone-less in a park. The trees have been relegated in interest for them by the high intensity repeated phone checking. Their minds have been desensitised.

Mindfulness

When the ability to sustain focus is built to a good level, mindfulness will become a powerful ally to meditation. In its basic sense, it is an awareness of the moments of the day as they unfold. A kind of ongoing meditative vigilance but the focus is generally on emotions, thoughts and feelings. The idea is to pause enough to observe these unconscious outputs before engaging with them. This is the mechanism that can detect, challenge and reroute auto-pilot behaviours that do not serve us well.

At first you will often simply forget to be mindful. It can take time to get a rhythm of pausing before engaging with thought or emotions. But you will soon start to notice that the unconscious talks a great deal. And much of it is not terribly important or wise. As we walk about there will be a kind of running commentary, peppered with judgements – why is that man letting his hair grow too long? Will the person in front of me let me pass? Wow – that lady has great legs. And so on.

I am impulsive by nature, so mindfulness is a powerful antidote. By way of illustration, when playing games of pool or snooker, before I have completely lined up my cue with the white and target balls, my unconscious will urge me to just get on and hit the ball. It can be **very** impatient. When I remember to be mindful, I can pause and observe this 'request' and let it fade, allowing me to align the shot now, free from interference. But the impulse will try again a few times. If I let if fade again each time it eventually gives up and I can play calmly and better than when I concede to the impulses.

When standing in a supermarket checkout queue, the inclination is to be impatient (again). To treat the queuing as necessarily a boring matter. Instead, I can observe that judgement, let it fade, and replace it with a meditation on my proprioception – the little bodily movements that keep me standing up. And I

17

can then often find a calm state of mind.

Sometimes mindfulness can catch the unconscious being sneaky. A number of days recently things went badly. So each time I started feeling a bit depressed. But I was mindful of that and I swiftly realised that these words – this judgement – was entirely emanating from my unconscious. So I let it fade and two seconds later the feeling of depression vanished. What might have cast a dark shadow across the day instantly vanished.

The benefits of mindfulness tend to outweigh the effort involved as is clear in that example. It is indeed hard to overstate how valuable this mind tool is. And what better way to make my point than by describing the biggest change it brought about for me. As a computer programmer for decades, there were often times when a 'bug' in the code proved elusive to chase down. For hours sometimes! I would thump the desk in a fit of temper, and regret the pain afterwards of course. The key method in preventing temper is not to express or suppress (it will manifest in another way later) but to defuse by reframing. I used mindfulness to observe the urge to lose my temper and challenged the need to do so. I realised that it would not help me fix the code. I was literally able in the mindful pause to see the anger that was blindly and impatiently urging me to thump the desk. Deflating the need for temper, it faded and I could return to the chore of seeking a code fix. After a few weeks, I trained myself not to lose my temper. Six years later I have not lost it since. Knowing that I will stay pretty calm even when things get tricky is a wonderful feeling.

A few more antidotes

The concept of acceptance is often misunderstood. Many see it as passivity when things go wrong, but it most certainly does not mandate that. We should accept that we have just dropped a bottle of expensive wine on the tiled kitchen floor. We accept that as a reality. Then we start to clean up the mess. Being mindful is key here – to give pause rather than explode in anger or frustration. Acceptance stops us conceding to unconscious urges to feel sorry for our loss also. And of feeling guilty of clumsiness. Instead, we calmly resolve and learn from what happened.

As a kind of variation on a theme, when we meet people – including strangers we may talk with – we accept how they are without judgement. The practice of non-judgement allows us to connect in a neutral but calm fashion. It can feel palpably different to those times we felt awkward as we did not like how someone was looking at us or that they stood too close. If they were a different skin colour you might observe some kind of recognition and an uncomfortable feeling of that difference. We see and accept difference and do not judge.

When people we meet feel accepted exactly as they are they tend to relax and open out in conversation. It is, as they say, a win-win situation. But not in a competitive sense. More in a connecting, collaborative sense. When we connect in a non-judgemental way we connect better and learn more and expand our horizons. And can make new friends.

Equanimity is a more subtle Buddhist notion. But not so easy to adopt. It essentially means that we accept pain and illness and relationship problems and many other things without buying into the 'flavour' of hardship or suffering that our unconscious appends to our problems. When we just accept the reality that we have torn our hamstring and just go with the flow, we are lighter. The pain can then start to feel like an attachment – a fringe matter.

As we navigate each day, the unconscious drive to preserve our life also seeks to expand and enhance it whenever it can. It can also create attachments as it does this. We feel pleasure and want to hold onto it so eat another piece of cake. We love the new TV and now want a new car. We can attach to success in sport and create tension in the process – playing matches with the result as focus can compromise performance as we can get too tight when things go wrong. Attaching is a kind of clinging. Instead we enjoy what might give pleasure but expect the pleasure to eventually fade and simply let go.

A new mindset

We are near the end of this little journey into understanding our mind. Many things have necessarily been omitted in order to focus on the conclusion that I will now draw.

This new mindset that can radically change the way you live your life.

It asks that you see yourself only as conscious awareness. To treat your body and unconscious as separate from your awareness, even though you have responsibility for your body! You are urged to treat them in a detached manner, along with the feelings, emotions and thoughts they send into your awareness.

You use mindfulness as much of each day as you can to observe this separation.

If you are reminded that you have a dark side, for example, then see also that you do not – you are simply aware of how that darkness manifests in the detached unconscious and body. The darkness is not part of your awareness.

A most difficult part of this separation is that there are most certainly entirely valid thoughts and urges to action that arrive from the unconscious. But validated and heeded by mindfulness scrutiny.

We treat all that comes from the unconscious as potentially questionable.

We are awareness that pays heed to and is responsible for the brain and body that is its transport. We are light in this awareness when freed from that tight coupling and subservience to all that the unconscious throws at us. We respond to what matters only.

This lightness of being frees us up to see and embrace the world. To connect more deeply with others, seeing their view of life more clearly.

I highly recommend that you try this mindset for a few days. That should be enough for you to start seeing why it is so wise a path to take.

Maybe a sample of my own experience as I grow this mindset will inform.

A rare day of constant clear blue sky with barely a breath of wind saw me set off for Cardiff city centre bus station. A notably painful journey with very sore right knee. I am aware of the pain and ensure I do not aggravate my knee. But I do not feel emotionally hampered in any way.

I arrived at the station to learn that the X2 bus I wanted to take to Cowbridge did not start there. The place I was directed to had no bus stop signs at all for an X2 bus. What a wasted journey I thought. Except I was aware that it was not my aware conscious that was making that comment. I was just receiving this judgement from my unconscious. And I chose most swiftly not to heed it. Besides, I had a very, very rare clear head – most days I have tension headaches for hours – and realised I was simply enjoying looking up at fabulous buildings bathed in sunshine sporting the most wondrous carvings. I was again living in the moment. That is the best we can get wherever we travel to. My attention to my awareness was a liberator for me again.

Child's play

The deeply under–estimated value of learning from play

There are so very many benefits of undirected child play that you might imagine that it would be the focal point of early schooling. Sadly here in Britain, it is pushed to one side as a trivial, inconsequential matter.

A reason why we do not value raw play is not just because we have forgotten quite how valuable it was to us (if we were lucky enough to have been given that freedom to play when young), but because we never consciously registered the benefits at the time. As we developed through play, we were fundamentally not mindful of how it was transforming us.

Since our memories of play tend to be pretty superficial, so we label play as being the same. This is a deeply sad situation, and one that explains in part (only in part) why the likes of Government Education Secretaries want children to buckle down and set about the 'business' of education as early as possible. They, like us, no longer see play as a deep and profound education in itself.

The Scandinavians, however, do. Formal education rarely starts before the age of 7 in these countries. However, rather than take their lead, we are increasingly influenced by the exam success of Asian countries where play is extremely marginalised and minimised. We are informed of their academic success, but not of the damage to health and development their lack of play creates.

The intention with this article is to solidify that argument – to show how extremely valuable and vital play is to normal, healthy child development.

Post war Britain

The lack of material things in the immediate post-war era saw child creativity at its peak. Bomb sites, for example, were exciting adventure grounds, where risk was embraced as a natural thing.

In comparison, life now is sterile, pre-packaged and often squeezes out any creativity. Children are like prisoners in the system, their voice rarely heard, and their personal development through natural play rarely recognised. Commercial interest in, and exploitation of, children sabotages a healthy development.

Paradoxically, the *freedom* that many children had in the 1950's was coupled with *responsibility* – the two are contingent on each other and the children instinctively knew this, each looking out for each other. Play was not just indulgence but cultivated care.

In that now long lost golden era, children would learn first hand about birds and animals, keenly reading further in books to enhance their understanding, acting like mini-scientists. They owned their agenda – it was not foist upon them in the sterile environment of school or a house with electronic gadgets.

Allowing cars to swamp the landscape and squeeze outdoor play has been one of the great unchallenged failures of many societies.

The value of play

In their group play, children learnt the value of *collaboration* rather than the competitive way of life that has been promoted in current times. Teacher or school led play is often competitive in nature rather than collaborative exploration. When play is adult driven, pecking orders appear amongst the children, just as they do in constrained animals.

Play strengthens the immune system. Conversely, the lack of exposure to dirt, for example, is seen as a potential cause in the rise in conditions such as asthma in the modern sterile world. But the sense of autonomy and self-empowerment that free play fosters is a powerful immune system strengthener.

Children develop a sense of self when they see themselves playing with others. The happiest people are those who can rely on their own resources. Rich and varied free play can cultivate that.

Early understanding in children is often in the form of polar opposites such as good/evil, love/hate and cruel/kind as they start with such broad concepts in order to build a large framework. Yet adults try to tone down what they teach and bombard them with details that the children are not ready for yet.

Directed play with pre-determined outcomes leads to frustration in children and greater unhappiness. Note here, then, the failure of construction sets with a single target model to build. It constrains rather than liberates.

Play is essentially 'practice for life'. And it is likewise essential to healthy development because of its experiential nature. Through play, the child becomes an active creator of their own learning, not a passive recipient of someone else's ideas.

Such hands-on learning and experiencing of life through activities such as play are vital since the human brain is not-preprogrammed as much as it is in animals. We have to acquire what is to be known about our particular environment and that is best done first hand.

Optimal play has a balance between assimilation (acquisition of knowledge) and accommodation (adaptation to circumstance). Amongst many others, Dr. Stuart Brown states that play is central to child development. It is a chastening statistic that about 90% of convicted murderers had abnormal or limited play time as children.

In rough and tumble play, children learn to limit their strength and aggressive impulses – the jostling cultivates social skills yet it can look ugly to adults. Another example of an inability of adults to look back to their youth with any real certainty or true clarity.

Children become democratic, agreeing roles of play, even if they do break the rules every so often.

The pleasure of play subordinates the ego as children enter a state of social harmony with their friends. Play teaches us about the perspective of others as the dynamics of activities flex around the ever changing needs of each within the play-group. But the very act of playing takes us out of ourselves – we become a part of a group and this alone is very beneficial to health. The egocentric, narcissistic converse is clearly bad for all to see.

The mental flexibility and adaptability play inculcates is mirrored by the physical flexibility that is also required. By contrast, those who had little play as a child are often rigid and mechanical in both mind and body.

> *In play the emergent self is revealed. Outer play becomes inner resource. The narrower the spectrum of choice, the more blinkered our thinking is likely to become. Playful adult thinkers can 'think outside of the box'.*

Recreating the real world

The word recreation literally means a *time of recreating*. When children copy adult behaviour, they start to feel what adults feel. No words can ever transfer to them that feeling – this experiential education is *qualitatively* different from adult bestowed education.

Having the opportunity to experience the real world – to go into the countryside and see the bird in the nest, to feel a clump of mud in your hand – is impossible to replicate in language.

Play is not limited to recreation or exploration. It is also a truly vital outlet for thoughts and feelings. A failure to provide such a release valve through play can create life-long problems.

Parents may be concerned about a child playing a sad game, but this often means that the child is reliving something that caused their upset, in order to come to terms with it. This reliving is especially troublesome for adults to understand when it follows trauma – children repeatedly relive aspects of trauma and it can freak adults out. The very same adults who may have a bad habit of hiding away such feelings and letting them fester.

Children who play doctors and nurses are less resistant to the effects of medical procedures and recover faster from them.

Ponder that one point. Truly ponder it.

Imaginary friends

Imaginary friends are often frowned upon by adults because, again, they cannot equate with them. But they have been shown to reduce aggression in boys and generally lower anxiety levels, increase happiness and generate more positive attitudes to life.

The more a child imagines, the happier they will be. Albert Einstein valued his gift of fantasy above his technical reasoning abilities. He believed that to make a child clever required the telling of fantasy stories, liberating the mind to be able to transcend barriers and convention. Fantasy is a benign, secure way to understand the world.

Adults actually do have a form of play their whole lives – in their dreams. Here, the rules are broken, and matters unfold in an unprescribed manner.

It is now well established that the passivity of TV kills creativity. The television becomes a weak *proxy* for experience. Likewise, toys are now so-often uni-functional, defining the role of the child – taking that decision away from the child, making them passive. Too many toys kills proper play – a herd mentality can then take its place.

By contrast, a discrete observer at Ringwood Waldorf school witnessed no less than 54 themes exercised during 17 observed hours of child play over a period of 11 days. These themes included diverse matters such as a cheese factory, and entertaining lots of visitors.

> *He loved his teddy for reasons other than its outward form*

Play as expression

Play can also be a form of expressive art for children. It does indeed have some of the quintessential features associated with adult creativity.

Symbolic play, where a bucket can become a hat, a chair-back or a letter box has been shown to enhance language development.

Learning language through play

Like a lot of child development, language evolves with broad brush strokes – approximations – subject to repeated refinement when deemed appropriate by the child. An iterative process that proceeds at different rates and times for different children, so testing at specific ages is more likely to reveal this varying time-scale more than varying ability or 'progress'. Sadly, politicians setting education curricula fail to understand such realities.

A child talking about 'bouts' confused his parents. Eventually, it transpired that the child mistook roundabout to mean a form of bout – that there could be square bouts also, for example. It was incorrect in the eyes of the adult, but for that child, very meaningful. The child was trying in his own way to understand one of the quirks of the adult world. Correcting the child in this literal play with words would have been very wrong.

When children learn, their approximations are good enough for them to get by and understand. They evolve with time, but adults want children to get to where they are – to do things with complete precision – yet forget the journey they took to get there. They need only remind themselves that each unrecognised word in a book becomes ever more understandable each time it is encountered, and that they are as happy with the intermediate, partial understanding as children are with theirs.

Forcing formal education when children are not ready damages growth – children become old before their time. Early pressures mean that children are :

> *"... failing to thrive emotionally, and becoming less resilient"*

Modern life is largely bereft of free play for children – it is narrowing down to sports play, work, and 'being entertained'.

Norman Douglas in 1916 :

> *"It all comes down to this. If you want to see what children can do, you must stop giving them things".*

Balancing Act

A simple but intriguing novelette

Dora O'Hallaghan, the grey haired lady at the Ashram Convenience Store turned to get a half bottle of Vodka from the shelves of alcohol behind her. She did so slowly enough to give her slightly anxious customer just enough time to furtively take a bar of extra creamy Galaxy chocolate from the counter, and slide it into his pocket. Dora was a kindly lady, and would never have suspected an act of theft so brazen as this. She was completely oblivious to the heist, asking only for the money for the alcohol.

Outwardly calm, but inwardly beaming at his success, Vincent Axiom made a rapid exit from the shop, smuggling the illegally gained prize in his coat pocket. When far enough away from the shop, he unwrapped and bit into the chocolate. The creamy taste erupted into his mouth, enveloping him with a deliciously warm, relaxed feeling, submerging any thoughts of guilt.

But all was not quite right. In his haste to leave the store, only now did he realise that he had been short changed by the lady. He was in a good mind to go back and complain, but even he was just too aware of the hypocrisy of such an action.

Damn. How could he have been so stupid.

Alas, things were to take one more bad turn that day. Or, more correctly, his stomach was to take a turn. Whilst the chocolate had left a nice taste in his mouth, it had not done the same to his stomach, and he retired to sleep curled up into the foetal position, with a bucket beside his bed. He felt awful, yet mindful enough to wonder why buckets always seem to have that nauseating bleached smell.

He also wondered quite how a sublimely delicious bar of chocolate could have messed up his insides so much. Or maybe it was the curry he had had for lunch?

Yeas, that's it, the Hunjuraj Palace Tandoori Indian restaurant would no longer be receiving his custom, that is for sure. Oh no- daddy-oh, no! They would be certain to suffer a serious loss of income as a consequence. Dora never noticed her monetary mistake.

Enid and Henry

Enid climbed the stairs to wake up her husband Henry. This couple were in their early 50's, still as much in love as in their courting days. She was relatively sprightly, but encumbered most of her days helping her husband who was heavily handicapped by rheumatoid arthritis. This condition swells the limbs, severely limiting movement, to the point where someone afflicted as much as Henry becomes housebound.

She knocked on the door.

"I've brought your breakfast up – you awake yet?" she asked. "Yup" he replied. When she entered the room, something was not quite right. Henry was sitting upright in the bed with a big smile on his face. Whilst this would be an ordinary matter for you and I, for Henry it was not.

"Thought I'd surprise you. I know it's hard for you to lift me up so I did it all on my own today." he explained.

Except that he had not done that for at least five years.

Enid was happy in a calm, gentle kind of way, preferring to enjoy this unexpected upturn in Henry's health rather than puzzle over its origin. However, Henry was undoubtedly happier – a small achievement like this was going to fuel an upbeat mood for the remainder of the day. Enid sat on the edge of the bed, and they talked with a lightened mood. Neither mentioned the strangeness of his newly acquired mobility for neither wanted to break the tranquility of the moment.

Sarah

Allegiances in Sarah Troutman's class were clearly divided between the Chelsea, Manchester United, Liverpool and Arsenal fans and the real football fans. Whilst Sarah saw herself as a true blue Chelsea fan, if truth be told, she was swayed more by their recent success than any affinity with football in that particular part of London.

What set her aside from her cohorts, however, was her deeply held Christian beliefs.

So it was pretty inevitable that one day she would be found kneeling down, praying to God for Chelsea to win one more match, and thereby regain the Premiership title from their fierce rivals, Manchester United.

She prayed :

> *"You know how good I try to be God. I only normally pray for the good fortune of others, so can I ask just once for something for myself?*
>
> *Actually, it is not even for me – it is for my football team. They really, really want to win the league. Manchester United have won it so many times, it must be time that Chelsea won again.*
>
> *Please, please, I'll go to church more often. Just this one request"*
>
> *"Thank you Lord for listening to my prayer."*

Both Chelsea and Manchester United lost on the last day of the season, allowing Liverpool to win the league for the first time in decades. Sarah was none too pleased.

Matthew

Matthew Bradman worked in Japan, monitoring seismic activity on the island of Honshu, underneath which the Eurasian and Pacific tectonic plates overlap.

He was principally employed to look for trends in the behaviour of these indescribably large lumps of matter, trying as best as he could to predict any possible volcanic or earthquake activity that can result from the abrasion of the plates with each other.

These huge plates are essentially a law unto themselves, choosing almost arbitrarily when to jostle their shoulders against each other, often giving false alarms. If you evacuate a city when nothing ensues then you're in big trouble. However, we've all seen what happens when an earthquake happens with no prior warning.

However, Matthew was noticing a new pattern of tectonic behaviour. It was unlike any he had seen in his twelve years in the job. The inter-plate noise was actually gradually reducing.

This sounded like good news of course, but his experience told him otherwise. This might instead mean the lull before the storm, much like the suddenly, unexpected receding waters on a beach that signal the imminent arrival of a tsunami.

So he went to amber alert, and cancelled his upcoming holiday. You see, Matthew was very dedicated to his job, and was somewhat worried about the possible ramifications of this new discovery. He had to be extra vigilant in the days and weeks ahead, and could not enjoy a holiday in such circumstances.

Seagulls

"Why is it that we can never find anywhere to park? The council are forever restricting roads to residents only. They complain about the big out of town supermarkets, but we cannot use the local shops because we just cannot park"

Phyllis said all this in frustration to little George, her 8 year old grandson, not for his benefit but simply because someone had to hear what she wanted to say.

"Ah, here we go, at last!" she said as she homed in on a gap in a row of parked cars.

That she straddled both a double yellow line and the zigzag that preceded a pedestrian crossing clearly did not register in her mind. With the target of parking achieved, off she strode, poor George's little legs struggling to keep up with her.

She knew that it was safe of course to infringe parking regulations like this, because council cutbacks had made traffic wardens an almost invisible breed.

However, Phyllis' car was bright red, precisely the colour that most readily caught the attention of a flockette of three sharp-eyed seagulls with some excess baggage to unload.
Whoosh, and Phyllis' car was now pebble dashed. The seagulls were proud of their accuracy, and would have smiled if their beaks had let them.

Smiling, however, was not the first thought that sprung to her mind when Phyllis returned to her now multi coloured Mini Coupe.

Ginger

It was very dark now, and therefore a good time to scout along the lane that lay between Alberta Terrace and Calgary Drive. The rear gardens were unusually equipped with low privet hedges rather than high fences or walls, affording Dave 'Ginger' Roberts full view of the rear of each house. He needed his torch light, however, as the lane had no lighting.

He saw a house without lights, extending to an outhouse with a flat roof. That would do. He checked both ways to make sure that he was alone, and then eased the back gate latch open, making sure it shut quietly behind him.

He tiptoed along the path, with that heightened sense of awareness that the seasoned criminal develops. He was vigilant like a cat approaching its prey, not wishing to make its presence known.

As he had hoped, the top-right bedroom window was slightly ajar – an open invitation that he believed entirely legitimised his planned intrusion. If they're going to make it easy for you to get in, then they'll learn a hard lesson. You see, even burglars have to justify what they do to themselves.

Still in cat mode, he climbed onto the bin, up onto the flat roof, along in a crouch, ever so carefully easing the window open before slipping inside. He had checked first that the room was empty.

Mr and Mrs Summers were out enjoying themselves. They had left the hall light on, but this was not visible from the rear. He had entered their son's room, and moved quickly downstairs to the lounge. He had a 35 litre rucksack, enough for a tasty iPad or X-Box. The LED TV was tempting, but just too big.

He scanned the room, then shuffled through the drawers of the display cabinet. Much to his surprise, he found a jewellery box and a wallet.

His luck was in.

He tipped the box contents into the lower section of his rucksack, and zipped it tight. He rifled through the wallet, extracting around £120 in five and ten pound notes into his pocket. As he dropped the wallet, three photographs slipped out of the middle, windowed section. They landed onto the table face-up.

Underneath the TV was a Blu-Ray player. This was indeed a very lucky strike. A good day.

You have to remember that these things were not for himself. Any burglar of reasonable experience had all the electronic equipment he needed. He would sell his ill-gotten gain at the car boot sale on Sunday morning, and be set up for a week of beer and the odd spliff.

As he untangled the wires from the Sony Blu-Ray player, he kept his ears open for any tell-tale sign of humans. And that also meant other burglars.

After slipping the player into the main part of his rucksack, he scanned the kitchen before returning to the lounge on his way back upstairs. As he passed through the lounge, his eye caught the upended wallet on the table. He sat down and looked at the photos. Obviously, the couple not only had a good camera, which he had yet to find, but also very pretty children.

One photo was of the family. All were beaming except the husband, who looked somewhat sad. He wondered why they kept that particular photo. Maybe it was the only one taken on that day, and the memory of the day was more important than his downbeat appearance.

It was not like Ginger to linger.

Here he was, in the middle of a burglary, and he was looking over family belongings. Not only that, but he was getting deeply distracted, trying to work out why the husband was sad.

He tried to picture this man when he arrived home later that night. That sad expression came to his mind. Poor bugger, he thought to himself!

"Don't get soft now, Ginge" he said to himself.

But having felt a change of mindset, he saw for the first time what he was doing. No, not the stealing itself. But what the stealing did to people. They would come home and feel more than their losses. They would feel abused. How could he not have seen this before? What was going on? Why was he doing this?

He ripped open the rucksack, and tipped the Sony player out onto the sofa. He removed the jewels from the zipped compartment, placing them next to the player. He withdrew the notes from his pocket, and placed them next to the jewellery box. He returned to the kitchen, and scribbled on the wipe clean board that he was sorry for invading their house.

He felt genuinely sorry that he had no time to leave tidily.

He sped upstairs, through the window, onto the roof and down into the garden, leaving as quietly as he had arrived, but otherwise quite a different person.

As he started walking home, his head bowed low, he decided to check how many houses along the road he was. He then marched that same number along the house fronts so that he could find out the number of the house he had infiltrated.

You see, later that day, he would write a letter to Mr and Mrs Summers, even though his letter would not be addressed to them by name of course. They were an anonymous target of his petty theft, and he was now able to see such theft for what it was. He felt a strange mix of emotions, having already decided to go on the straight and narrow. He was going to have to find some other way of paying for his vices, which was a pain, but writing the letter would end this sordid time of his life.

He felt sweetly elevated in mood by his new enlightenment.

Leonard

Some car repair garages have unenviable, but justified reputations for cowboy repairs, and Thomson's Auto Repairs was no exception. So it was well within their capabilities to overlook minor, trivial details, like, you know, a hand brake that was teetering on the edge of failure.

Which is exactly why Leonard Smith should never have parked his car on a hill. Indeed, this was a very bad idea. Some minutes after he had left the car to go shopping, the very blustery conditions in combination with the rush of a monster Tesco lorry was just enough to ease his car into an irreversible downward descent. Ever so slowly at first, as the hand brake hung in there, gallantly trying to carry out its simple role to the very end. But the car was soon out of control, the handbrake now ineffective. It headed unmanned towards the busy shopping street below, and a morass of unsuspecting shoppers.

It careered towards a line of pedestrians at a bus stop along the way, but somehow managed to stay on track on the road. A few gave it puzzled looks, wondering exactly what the driver was doing, completely out of sight. By the time the road started levelling out, the car had picked up a fair speed, with the handbrake now useless in stopping its advance.

Thora Jones was 90, and had an unfortunate habit of stepping onto zebra crossings without checking that vehicles had noticed her. She ambled ever so slowly across, assuming in all her innocence that cars should stop as a matter of course. And yes, normally they did. But now we are talking about a car without a conscience, speeding straight towards the oblivious old lady.

Witnesses said afterwards that they could hear the squeal of brakes as the car abruptly came to a halt precisely at the edge of the zebra crossing. And that Thora remained unaware of her very lucky escape. The Police were called, but dismissed all witnesses as unreliable. They towed the car away, and contacted the Swansea DVLA to inform the driver of the whereabouts of his vehicle.

When Leonard returned later that day to go home in his car, he was somewhat disappointed to find that it had been 'nicked'. When he later recovered the car, no explanation was provided as to what had happened to it.

So Leonard was left very puzzled and worse off to the sum of £125, the fee to reclaim his vehicle.

Enid and Henry again

What started out as a little game each morning gradually progressed, as Henry slowly regained feeling and mobility in his limbs. The swelling reduced, and he was able to make his own way downstairs, revelling in the delight of afternoons relaxing in the garden as Enid pottered around weeding and planting flowers and shrubs.

Whilst Enid was delighted in this strange change of events, she still felt that Henry should seek a medical opinion to try to explain his health reversal. Henry was reluctant because he believed that his positive outlook was influencing his condition, and that Doctor Jones was never very sympathetic with his plight at the best of times.

But Enid won her way and a series of tests were carried out on Henry. The results duly baffled the medical profession. Degenerative conditions did not reverse as seamlessly as they appeared to be doing in Henry's case.

Had he been taking any additional supplements they asked? Taking more exercise than normal? They insisted that he must have been doing something to reverse this situation.

And for once, they did indeed hear his tales of positive thinking.

The "Power of the mind" he told them.

But they only listened so as to humour him, and recorded a verdict yet again of

"Spontaneous remission" in their notes without ever stopping to wonder what was really going on. They were medics – they only worked on things that were wrong with people. When their patients got better, they were no longer interested, which was a profoundly sad attitude of course, denying them the opportunity to learn about good health.

One day, rather a long time in the future, they would learn to realise that investigations into "spontaneous healings" would open the door to new realms of healing knowledge.

Catherine and Charlie

British comedy rarely survives the trans-Atlantic journey to the United States of America mostly because it so often portrays its cast as self-effacing. With their euphoric, upbeat focus on individual achievement, to lampoon yourself if you are American is just not funny.

This British habit extends to the alternative naming of institutions. So it is that the 'Crown and Sceptre' pub, tucked away in a side street behind Upper Regent Street in Central London is better known by Catherine Blobby and her cohorts as the 'Hat and Stick'.

In addition to her unfortunate name, poor Catherine also had to suffer the somewhat more tangible fates of being pig-ugly, and as thick as two planks. Two very short but substantial planks. Not only that, she was also blessed with a naturally tactless nature. A diplomat she was not!

We find her today in dialogue with her best friend Charlie, a very tolerant, understanding lady, herself beset with certain 'problems', probably best not delved into here.

"I noticed it on Monday last week," Catherine said to Charlie.

"I've checked loads of photos and my jaw is *definitely* not so long."

"What the hell are you on about, Cath? We meet for the first time in over a week and you start talking rubbish again" Charlie replied.

"Sorry Charlie, but you've got to believe me – just look. Look now – see how my face is rounder."

Charlie scrutinised Catherine's face and was not convinced. Part of the reason is that people in general are not terribly observant. They delude themselves into thinking they are, but they miss much more than they would like to think they do.

Catherine rummaged into her bag and lifted out an envelope containing two photographs of herself. Although not taken at the same angle, it was evident to the layman that her face had changed shape. But faces do not change shape just like that. Well, not as quickly as this without surgery.

Which explained Charlie's incredulity. She gazed at these photos, but her mind kept drifting off.

"And," Catherine continued, "men look at me more often".

But Charlie was not really listening. One of the reasons she was able to be tolerant with Catherine was that she frequently drifted away into a different world, oblivious to whatever Catherine was talking about.

They upped and left, Catherine irritated by Charlie's indifference. As they departed, Catherine's eye caught that of a young man who had just entered. The visual embrace lasted a few seconds before the man held the door open for them.

"What was that all about?" Charlie asked Cath when out of earshot.

"OK, maybe *now* you understand what I am on about! I look different, and men are starting to notice. Oh, and I've started reading books as well."

"You never read books. You've always said you hated them."

"No idea why, but I can kinda understand them better now" Catherine ventured, as she ambled along the road.

Charlie walked alongside her wondering what on earth was going on in the mind of her friend. This just might be one crazy thing too many for her to cope with.

Sarah again

A week after the end of the football season, Sarah was to be found with tears rolling down both of her cheeks. The television programme she was watching was covering the devastation wreaked on an African village by the continuing drought conditions. No rain had fallen in fully eight months and all but one of the water wells had dried up.

The sheer reality of the situation was made graphic by the televisual imagery, but Sarah barely needed that. From her privileged position of comfort in Britain, she was very aware of the plight of the villagers. And the only thing she felt she could do to help now was to pray for rain for them. She knelt down by her bed, and spoke rather than thought her prayer :

"Dear God, the situation in Africa is very bad now. Please, please can you help the rains fall so that the people don't die a miserable death? Please God hear my prayer. Amen."

She paused, head bowed, hoping that this respect would give her prayer an extra sense of power.

As she was about to stand up, the room went very, very quiet. She paused, sitting on the end of her bed. She heard no sound of cars, of birdsong. Gone was the tinkle of trees rustling. She could not say for sure if she could even hear the sound of her own heart. But it was not a cold, oppressive quiet. It had a gentle calmness.

Until, that is, she heard a voice speak.

Thank you Sarah.
The situation is in hand – I will help them shortly.

She looked around and could see no one. "Who was that? You're frightening me."

Please do not fear.
You will learn more soon.
This is all I can say now.

Sarah asked if she was hearing the voice of God, but the voice was no longer to be heard. Instead, the calm quiet disappeared as fast as it had arrived.

She ran from her room, raced down the stairs, and jogged to the All Saints Methodist Church a couple of streets away.

It was a Wednesday afternoon, but there was a chance that the Vicar would be there. She had to tell someone that she had heard the voice of God. At least, this is what she hoped she had heard.

She was in luck, finding Reverend John Vectis preparing a sermon for the upcoming Sunday. She approached him with an explosion of words that she of course had to repeat at a measured pace. John was not a man to be rushed. Oh no.

However, he was a good listener, waiting until the end of the second run of her monologue before speaking.

"This is what happened, my child?" he asked.

"Yes, of course" she replied.

"Have you been studying hard for your exams? Maybe you are starting to hear things?"

"You don't believe me, do you? I guessed you wouldn't."

"But what you are saying is very profound. You know this."

They spoke further but never in accord. You see, it is not possible for the ego of even a humble, deeply religious man such as John to countenance the possibility that someone else would be spoken to directly by God. He himself had received guidance from the almighty, but always via mere signs and other subtle means. He always had to interpret God's meanings in the things that happened around him.

He felt short-changed that here was this young lady claiming to have been chosen to hear His voice in all its glory. This was not right – if God was going to speak, then surely only one of the most devoutly religious of his flock should be the blessed recipient.

He hastened to clear his mind of these selfish thoughts, and humoured Sarah, in as kind a manner as he could muster in the circumstances, allowing her to hold onto the dream that she had been the chosen one. Yes, that's right, this would help her grow into a fine upstanding Christian woman.

Sarah bought his words readily, allowing herself to feel so special that she floated on air for days.

Greg

Gregory Julian Roberts was known by friends as Greg, and by his enemies as Caveman, probably because of his somewhat primitive appearance and behaviour. And he was known by his younger sister Emily as the Evil Bully.

His view, as the eldest child, was that he had to keep Emily in check. She, of course, did not share this view. Naturally, she hated the way that he treated her with disdain and contempt.

On this particular day, Greg had endured a very annoying time at school that had included a double Maths lesson. To Greg, Mathematics was a form of torture that he never grasped. So Emily became the inevitable outlet for him to let off steam.

"Gimme some of your chocolate" he ordered his sister.

"No – get yer own." she defiantly replied.

He tried to grab it, but she was too fast. So brute force was needed. He grabbed her arm and twisted it behind her back. The half eaten chocolate bar dropped to the floor. He grabbed it and pinched her leg for good measure.

As he did so, he felt her pinch his leg.

"You cheeky fing, pinching back. Fink you're tough?"

"What cho on about, I didn't touch ya" she replied.

He pinched her again, and felt her pinch him back. Except that he could now see that her arms were indeed not moving. He slapped her leg smartly, and felt a smack on his leg at exactly the same time.

"You got some special powers now or sumfink?" he asked her.

"What cho on abou'. I ain't done nufink." she exclaimed.

Being somewhat retarded of mind, it took rather a lot of attacks on poor Emily before Greg realised that whatever he did to her happened back to him with equal measure. But when the penny eventually did drop, he left her alone. For the next few days, he warily kept a comfortable distance. When Emily realised that she was no longer likely to be arbitrarily bullied, her attitude to Greg lightened up.

She stopped teasing him, and felt a resurgence of sisterly love. This in turn had a reciprocal effect on Greg, and over the coming weeks, they started warming to each other.

Whether it was this closer bonding, or a lingering fear about that strange day,

Greg never hurt her again.

John

Two days later, John Vectis was sitting comfortably at home watching the television. And for once, some good news lightened the fare – a monsoon was bringing much welcome relief to large parts of Western Africa. The BBC had commentary from the same village they reported on two days ago. The dusty scene of drought shown then was now replaced by an altogether different one, where children were dancing bare-foot in the rain.

It took a few moments for John to be nudged by this news into remembering what Sarah had said to him in great excitement on Wednesday. Could this really be the same village she had been talking about? Instinctively, he realised that this was indeed the most likely reality, and a deep feeling started brewing in the pit of his stomach.

Is it really possible that God would speak to someone like Sarah, and then carry out her prayer? We are all equal in the eyes of the Lord, but surely he and the countless other religious dignitaries around the World were better recipients of His almighty attention?

He had to contact her.

Fortunately, details of all the regulars at the church were held in the office, and he headed that way in all haste, swiftly finding Sarah's telephone number.

"This is Reverend John here. Is that Sarah?" he asked into his mobile phone.

"Hi John. That's very flattering, but no, it's her Mother. She's out at the moment. Was there anything special that I can help you with?" Megan replied.

"Thanks, but I really do need to speak to Sarah personally. When will she be back?"

"Actually, not that long. But you might want to ring her on her mobile since she passes the church on her way home."

Megan gave him Sarah's mobile number, and he immediately rang her. She agreed to meet with him, in maybe 20 minutes time, at the church. When she arrived, the roles now reversed, and it was his turn to be the energised, excited one. He explained about the monsoons, and as he did so, a serene, sweet smile slowly lit Sarah's face, giving her an angelic look.

For a while, they both sat there, allowing the impact of what they shared to start to fully dawn upon them.

"I'll take you home Sarah. Thank you so much for dropping by. I think you realise the importance of all this, and I trust that we can keep it to ourselves for the time being. Is that OK?" he said.

"Yes, yes, of course. Besides, I'm not sure anyone would actually believe me anyway" she replied, as she slipped out of the church.

"Do you want me to escort you home?" John asked as she left. "No, but thanks anyway."

When the last person had left the church, John sat in the rearmost pew, too humble to take a more advanced position, and prayed like he had not prayed before. He hoped, desperately hoped, that God would also talk to him.

But no quiet descended upon him. No tranquil voice entered his head.

Hospital

The Oncology Department of Birmingham Children's Hospital is necessarily a very sad place to the eyes of most visitors. Seeing someone afflicted by the latter stages of cancer is hard for anyone to take in. To see this in a young person magnifies this feeling enormously.

But today, Doctor Michael Brown entered the ward with a sprightly spring to his step. And an irresistible smile that his professionalism was unable to hide.

They had checked the scans of all eleven children in the ward. Checked again and again until there was no doubt.

"Hello Hannah, how are you feeling today?" he asked the 7 year old girl in the first bed.

"Hello Doctor Brown. I'm alright." she replied

"Do you miss being at home?"

"Of course I do. My bed is much nicer than this one."

"Do you want to go home then?"

41

"Can I? Am I better? Who is going to take me home?"

Doctor Brown left her side for a moment to usher in her parents. He had spoken to them earlier. They swung the curtain around little Hannah, allowing her parents some privacy to dress her. You could hear Hannah being hugged, and the soft whimpering sound of her Mother as she all but squeezed the life out of her only child.

Doctor Brown moved to the next child, and announced to her also that she may go home. But before he moved to the third bed, he noticed the anxious eyes of the nine other children were bearing down on him. This was not going to be so easy, he realised. He was going to have to break protocol, and make an announcement to all the children.

"You are all going to go home today. Your parents are outside waiting. You are all free from cancer. We do not understand why, but please just go home and enjoy your lives – you have all been wonderfully well-behaved patients."

He told Nurse Dickens to bring the parents in.

He left as they arrived, unable to cope with the surge in energy that permeated the ward.

Parents and children laughed and cried, emotions all mixed up.

Matthew again

"Bharami, did you get the trace file?" Matthew asked his Indian colleague by telephone.

"Yes I did," he replied "and normally I would understand your concern. But the trace signature does not follow any patterns I've seen before."

Bharami was one of a number of seismology contacts Matthew regularly used. Seismic behaviour was often best understood via the bigger picture – collating the pockets of information from around the World often furnished greater understanding of local behaviour.
"The trace is not just quiet, which can be worrying – it is actually declining – it is getting quieter. The seismic activity is diminishing. You can trust my confidence in this judgement because I too have recorded the same pattern in the Indian Ocean" Bharami said.

"We need to arrange a conference as soon as we can to get a grip on this. To say that this is an exciting development is something of an understatement. Are you available next week to meet up in Japan? I've been in contact with Horato in Kyoto and he tells the same story." Matthew replied.

"I'm busy until Thursday, but can free up the weekend if that's OK."

This was the first of a number of phone calls that helped coordinate the first emergency seismic conference since the 1995 Kyoto earthquake. Matthew thought it appropriate to meet at the epicentre of that quake.

Enid and Henry yet again

It was Enid's 53rd birthday party. As always, she anticipated a quiet day, and a big hug and kiss in lieu of a present from her housebound husband.

But this year was different. Henry had acquired so much mobility now that he had started meeting up at the allotment with his friends twice a week. Or at least this is what Enid had been led to believe. But Henry had split his allotted time, so to speak, in two. One day chatting at the allotment with his gardener friends, and the other working part time in a garden centre.

So he had earned enough money to be able to surprise Enid with a second hand sewing machine as a birthday present, one of those clever ones that can even embroider your name.

He had to explain, of course, that he had, well, sort of lied to her about his part time job.

"Oh Henry, why did you go and do such a thing for me? You big old softy!" she exclaimed.

"After all you've done for me, it was the very least I could have done as a small thanks" he replied.

"But I have another surprise for you as well. Gretchins, the garden centre, are going to let me work five afternoons a week, starting next month" he continued, and then had to placate Enid, who tried to insist that he take it easy instead.
You see, Henry was not lazy by nature, and had felt imprisoned by his crippling arthritis. He was a new man now, like a boy with his first pay-slip. And he wanted to live life to the full. If it meant a bit of discomfort from hard work, then so be it.

Not so many weeks later Enid also decided to return to work. Their joint incomes eventually earned them enough money to buy a caravan and set off on a tour of the Cotswold's and the Lake District. And, some months later still, they were able to fly to Canada to visit their daughter's family.

Geoffrey and Ben

Geoffrey Forde was a frustrated man. Having finally acquired all the acres of fertile land he had aspired to, his body was no longer able to manage them. He could plant seeds and tend to them, but the digging required a garden assistant. And yet another had just let him down.

So it was that he started walking to the shops in a sour mood, not least because it was terribly windy. His compromised body struggled in such conditions.

As he arrived at the junction of Peter Street and Chilcott Terrace, steering his body towards the former, a series of wind gusts kept pushing him towards the latter. He could get to the shops that way, but it was a longer journey. He tried to fight the wind, but finally had to concede and set off on the path less travelled.

His day of frustrations was not quite over. After a hundred yards, a tremendously powerful gust finally threw him off his feet. He stumbled forward towards Ben, a sharp-minded homeless man who had been watching Geoffrey's perilous advance. He sprung to his feet and broke the fall of Geoffrey with great aplomb. It made him feel good for the first time this day, of value rather than a social eye-sore many sadly see him as.

When Geoffrey realised what had happened, he was terribly grateful to Ben.

"Thank you so much. You saved me serious injury I feel."

"No problem" Ben replied "happy to be in the right place and time."

Geoffrey was now quite obviously aware of Ben strength, and had the insight to realise that he could be of great value employed doing the heavy digging work on his allotments.

And Ben was of course delighted to accept the offer, happy to be engaged in something meaningful, rather than a precarious pseudo-existence.

"You can sleep in the shed. It has a small night heater to keep it warm."

Both Ben and Geoffrey departed with raised spirits.

Locusts

Whilst Africa has historically been the most affected by infestations of pests, nearby Yemen had recently been bombarded by swarms of locusts that razed millet, rice and maize crops to the ground. Being relatively new to this form of attack, the impact had been devastating to the Yemen people, with many families crippled by malnutrition.

The effectiveness of pesticides had reduced in the last few years, with new breeds of locusts blatantly disregarding the rules and failing to die.

But this year, the crops were robust, and the expected locusts simply did not turn up. Maybe they had seen tastier fare elsewhere, but that seemed most unlikely. Or maybe the anti- locust tribal dances were being particularly efficacious for once.

The locals, were, let us say, cautiously ecstatic. And somewhat plumper than you would normally find them. Which is to say that they almost looked healthy.

The governments of the World were of course very much aware of unusual events like this, and were keeping a close eye on matters. They were looking for a common theme, as this was not an isolated incident, but they only had conjectures so far.

Dr Rowan Williams

Dr Rowan Williams, the Archbishop of Canterbury and head of the Church of England, had extensive responsibilities that were of course not confined to the shores of Great Britain. Sometimes, this weighed heavily on his shoulders.

Fortunately, apart from the occasional ill-judged comment, the head on these shoulders was a wise one.

On this particular day, which would be unlike any day before in his illustrious career, he was to be found researching material for a forthcoming Diocesan Conference in Hereford. He sat alone at his computer, having for some time taken advantage of modern technology to simplify his work.

He looked out of the window, pondering the plight of the homeless, and noticed a slight cool descend over the room. It was accompanied by a gentle quiet, as the sound of birds outside faded into the background.

He slowly released himself from his train of thought to embrace this inexplicable calm. His mind was clear, free from chatter and emotions.

The calm was softly broken by a strong but smooth voice.

Good evening Rowan.

The same voice that had spoken to Sarah some days ago now.

Being of passive disposition, Rowan did not react to the voice, a voice that sounded from within his head. He was relaxed and receptive, and replied as if from Buddhist training in like fashion.

"I am fine. How are you?" he said, his eyes fixed upon the window, content to remain there, feeling no urgency to find the body that must surely accompany the voice.

I am fine.
Thank you for asking.

Rowan could sense something ethereal about the voice, something transcendental that was not really of this World. So he felt compelled to ask :

"Are you God?"

To which the voice replied :

Yes, that is the name by which you know me.

With the air still cool and calm, quiet and serene, Rowan sat and pondered this. He had been a key figure in various roles for his Church for many years now. The depth of his Christian faith was profound and unwavering.

But now he was apparently being spoken to by God with a clarity that mocked what he thought he had heard before. He was personally hearing the voice of the Almighty. And his heart was starting to race.

Minutes passed with no sound apart from the faster inhalation and exhalation of his breath.

"What do you want me to do, O Lord?" he eventually asked.

I ask of you a strange favour. I apologise that I do so this first time that we converse. I would like you to make arrangements with the British Broadcasting Corporation in London to present a television programme for International transmission.

The programme will be of ten minutes duration, to take place after the last scheduled discussion at the Group of 8 Summit in Geneva next month. It is my hope that you are sufficiently well respected by the BBC for them to approve such a programme.

You must tell the BBC that the programme will be of significant International interest, but the content must remain confidential until the very time of the transmission itself.

You will have rightly guessed that I will be present for this broadcast, but I cannot say more now about the nature of the content. I ask that you keep my attendance a complete secret from the BBC, your friends and even your family.

Rowan sat a while to absorb this request.

"O Lord, please let me ask you one question. What you request I will surely do. I would travel to the ends of the World for you. But to hear your voice for the first time, and to hear such a request just seems extremely odd. It is surely too demeaning that you should be asking me to help you.

Can you enlighten me, just a little?" Rowan pleaded.

You are a fine man Rowan, and you have said many times that God works in mysterious ways. For now, I would like this purported habit of mine to be sustained just a little longer.

Rowan confirmed that he would make the arrangements, for which he was thanked, and then left alone in deep contemplation.

He had a lot to think about.

Mark Thompson

"Can I please speak to Mark Thompson. I am the Archbishop of Canterbury" Rowan asked the BBC switchboard. For the second time.

The first time that he had been connected through, the switchboard operator replied that he himself was the Duke of Kent, and put the phone down in a fit of giggles.

"Putting you through now, sir" the operator said this time.

Mark Thompson was about as busy a man as Rowan, albeit with a schedule that was somewhat different. He did, however, tend to field calls from dignitaries, risking the odd prank call.

"Good morning Rowan, this is a pleasant surprise. How can I help you?" Mark proffered.

"Good day to you, sir. And may I take the opportunity of thanking you for a splendid range of programmes, still the best broadcaster in the World" Rowan replied, always preferring to flatter as a gentle way into dialogue with powerful men.

"I have a difficult request of you I am afraid. I would ask, no, implore, that you are able to schedule a ten minute programme for an important international announcement I would like to make. It must be held in Geneva, Switzerland in July as the last item on the agenda of the G8 summit."

"This is somewhat unusual, you do realise, Rowan. Can you give me a flavour of the message you need to give?"

"Actually, I cannot. I really am in no position to release any details whatsoever prior to transmission. I can only offer you two things …

… First that you will absolutely not regret the decision to proceed with the programme. And secondly, that as head of the Church of England, you can trust that my intentions are entirely honourable."

The line went quiet for a few moments.

"Excuse me a moment Rowan, I need to talk with the head of programmes. Can I call you back, or will you hold the line?" Mark asked.

"I'll hold. Please do not rush your decision. I understand that my request requires some thought."

But Mark did indeed agree to air this mystery programme, on the condition that the BBC had full marketing rights, and would be accredited as the producers. And of course it would be subject to approval from the organisers of the G8 summit. Not exactly an easy task, but Rowan had good powers of persuasion, and, most importantly, good contacts, so would readily be able to gain this approval.

Rowan accepted Mark's terms, and resumed his more traditional role as Religious leader rather than programme organiser. He heard no further word from God that day. He thought to tell God in a prayer exactly when the programme was due to go on air, but he assumed, quite rightly, that God would be fully aware of such matters.

Summit else

The position of Archbishop of Canterbury brought with it a great deal of international influence, and Rowan Williams was shrewd and open-minded enough to use this power to international benefit more than for elevating his own status.

So it was that the assembly of leading players in the Group of 8 most powerful countries at the Geneva summit was now supplemented by a strong representation of the leading figures of the World's diverse religions. Amazingly, this even included the Pope.

Most impressive, though, was how Rowan was able to attract these otherwise very busy figures without being able to tell them exactly what they would be witnessing or partaking in. Suffice to say, though, that his head was on the line if their mass attendance proved a disappointment.

The G8 representatives from the UK, USA, Canada, France, Germany, Japan, Italy and Russia were meeting for their annual 3 days of discussions on mutual and global matters, such as the environment, and the ever increasing divide between the wealthy nations and the so called 'Third World' nations.

These meetings regularly attracted heated protests, often simply because the actions agreed in many summits were mostly token, aimed more at deflecting criticism than in truly tackling the real problems that beset all but the G8 countries themselves.

The Geneva summit was much like those that preceded it, with the sympathy lavished on matters such as the perennial problem of AIDS in Africa rarely matched by tangible, meaningful promises. Always, the financial security of the G8 economies was carefully protected as a priority.

But this time, there were rumours circulating the activists sprinkled around the building in Geneva that something big was going to happen this year. The rumours were inconsistent, but widespread. Something special was indeed going to happen.

As the summit drew to an end on the third day, the atmosphere inside the building started reflecting that mood outside. The G8 representatives, the religious leaders and the audience were all increasingly wary that the final item on the agenda was the Summit summit, as it were – the pinnacle of the meeting – the icing on the cake.

The official line was for that a very special announcement would be made by an extra special guest. No details beyond this were provided, not even to the G8 reps.

The time eventually arrived, with the last discussion swiftly brought to an unusually premature close. The main lights faded out, leaving the whole building in near darkness, save for a few safety lights. A calm descended over all that were present.

The BBC cameras had started broadcasting, not really knowing what to expect. A deep but gentle voice began to speak. From this point onwards, the World would become a much different place.

The World listens

The voice spoke to those present and those Worldwide receiving the broadcast.

Good evening to you all. I am known to you most commonly by the name of God, or Allah.

A swell of emotion filled the room, but everyone remained remarkably quiet, transfixed by what they were hearing.

I must first apologise for taking this unusual measure to talk with you, my creatures. And I must also apologise for speaking in English. I believe that this is the most appropriate language for International broadcast.

I use the medium of television for very practical reasons. To communicate with all of you individually would take me far too long in my present condition.

As God spoke, the audience in the building remained transfixed in quiet shock. Those watching on televisions were reacting somewhat differently. Equally transfixed, but somewhat more noisily so.

I will first try to reassure you that I am who I say I am.

Such is the power of illusion in modern television, I am once again obliged to apologise – for the mechanism of this proof. Please bear with me, and please remain calm – no one will come to harm in what follows.

One by one, the G8 representatives slowly rose into the air to a height of about ten feet. The look on their faces was priceless, but they heeded God's word and remained composed.

At least mostly composed.

Please walk to the rear of the building.

Everyone had seen levitations on television, with raised figures sweeping across a stage. But no one had any doubt that these men walked as if on solid ground, tentatively at first, but with confidence gained, robustly striding towards the mains doors at the back, with clear air beneath their feet. At which point, they were gently lowered to the ground.

Once again, I apologise for the nature of this demonstration. I normally prefer to use my powers, slowly returning as they are, for the benefit of the needy. I would ask you to remain where you are please.

I have chosen to speak to you all for a number of reasons, the first of which is an apology, my third today. I deeply wish to apologise to you all for my absence for such a very long time.

When I explain this absence and other matters, you will likely have many questions to ask of me. I will try to answer some questions now, but time is limited. So I request of you, my creatures, to arrange another opportunity for me to talk to a mass audience.

A few minutes had elapsed of the scheduled ten minutes. The BBC, the organisers of the summit and the audience Worldwide desperately wanted this meeting with the Lord to be allowed to take its natural course, even if this took hours.

But God was the only voice that had spoken – not one person had uttered a single word. They were humbled by His presence. Most deeply in awe were of course the religious leaders, all to be found knelt in various supine postures of subservience on the floor.

Intermingled with this awe was, however, some discomfort. He had rather a lot to explain by describing himself as both God and Allah. For now, their subservience and sheer curiosity for more kept all from speaking.

But one voice broke the silence. It was Rowan, compelled in his role as event organiser as it were, to ask God if He was able to stay a while longer in order to ask questions.

"As your humble servant" he started, "I would like to request your presence just a little longer in order that we may ask questions of you now. To wait for another day would be too painful I fear."

Thank you for this request.

If the BBC are happy to continue broadcasting, I am happy to continue beyond the scheduled time.

A spokesman for the BBC swiftly gave the nod, and God continued.

There are dark forces that you know mostly as the devil or Satan. I have always fought these forces, but for the last few millennia, they have held me captive. I cannot describe in your terms this captivity, but suffice to say, it has left me with precious little energy or time to care for you, my creatures.

I believe that I am now mostly free from the grip of these satanic forces, and able once again to turn my attention to you all. I have started attending to various matters, some small, some large, but there is much more for me to do. So I ask of you to have patience with me.

I feel that I have said all that I need to say for now, and invite questions. I will limit this to one question per person from each of the key dignitaries in attendance here. I do so for economy of time, and ask that you do not feel that I am overtly biased towards people in a position of power. I select them for the likely succinctness and appropriateness of their questioning.

The World questions

The quiet that had overtaken the building was broken now by fervent chatter. The G8 delegates walked from the rear of the room to join the religious leaders. They briefly huddled in a group before Rowan broke away to speak to the audience and God.

"We humbly thank you for allowing us this time for questions. We will present our questions in no particular order, and hope that you can bear with us, for any clumsiness in the words we use, and the questions we ask" Rowan said.

"Since I am already speaking, I will be the first to ask a question of you, my Lord."

"We all believed that you, God, were all powerful. Yet you talk of a contest with Satan. Are there limits to your power?"

And God replied :

Thank you for your question. I am afraid that in my absence over centuries now, what has been recorded about me has become somewhat distorted and misconstrued. When faced with a larger than life power, the human tendency is to exaggerate. My powers are difficult to describe in your terms, but they are very much finite.

After Rowan thanked God for his answer, the Islamic representative was next to speak.

"You refer to yourself as both God and Allah. We Muslims are brought up to believe that there is only one Allah. That the God of Christianity is a fabrication. The Christian faith believes that Jesus is your son, and somehow he is you also. We believe that Jesus was a messenger for your word, but that Allah is a single God. Can you please enlighten me?" he asked.

> **You ask a very good question. However I answer, even though I tell the truth, will cause deep upset to many millions of people who hold misinformed views.**
>
> **It is sad to me, now that I am able to turn my attention back to the planet and all the life that tries to thrive but often struggles to live upon it, that the centuries of my absence has driven them into contradictory and opposing directions.**
>
> **But I must answer truthfully and must then deal with the aftermath. I ask of you to hold no grievance against your fellow man, woman or child, regardless of the errors in their thinking. They were in no position to be enlightened until now, and I make a fourth apology – that it has taken so long for me to speak to you as I do now.**
>
> **Jesus was indeed a messenger. He was a fine man, and I was able to help him promote a respectful life by enabling him to carry out healings and such like.**
>
> **He was not my son however, for I am but one entity. Call me God, Allah, or any of the other names you bestow upon me. I am just me.**

Gasps of surprise, shock and elation permeated the building. But these outbursts were swiftly dampened by the Islamic spokesman.

"Thank you, Allah, for your answer. Whilst Muslims will of course feel vindicated by what you say, I can sense that there is a deeper meaning to what you are telling us which transcends any new sense of superiority that the supporters of the Islamic faith might now feel over other faiths, and indeed over the atheists and agnostics of the world."

"I am allowed only one question, but I would like to take this opportunity to make one statement to the collected audience ...

You are in the presence of Allah. He is real insofar as we can hear his voice and sense his power. And I ask of the world to take this opportunity to forget our differences and join together as one in harmony. Our God is more real than ever, and will take us into a new world order. We miss this opportunity at our peril."

As he finished, his final words were drowned in a cascade of cheers and clapping hands, everyone to a man standing in unified appreciation.

The next to ask a question was the Japanese delegate.

"This is not easy for me, you understand" he started, speaking via an interpreter. "In common with many Japanese, I am an atheist, and now find myself talking with God. I have experienced enough today to have lost any doubt that you are who you say you are. But to come to terms with this is a struggle of great magnitude for me."

"There are many important questions that I should ask of you, a being that until this afternoon I categorically felt did not exist. But I am too humbled and also obliged to ask but one question. You are claimed to be perfect. Now that you are regaining your powers, will you make the world perfect?" he asked.

I thank you for your courage in facing me. I hope to show you in the coming years that I am not a force to fear. In answer to your question, just as I am not all powerful, I am not perfect. Those that describe me thus do so without much depth of thought.

If they were to follow through with their thinking, they would realise that the concept is meaningless to ascribe to an entity such as myself, just as it is to ascribe to many other things.

Ask a car maker to make the most perfect car in the world, and they will hesitate. They will ask if it should be powerful, or fast, or efficient, or attractive. What is perfect for one person is not so for another. Perfection is sensed in a thing, not an invariant attribute of that thing. When dealing with humans, compromise permeates everything. It is a way of life. If I were to be perfectly fair with everyone on the planet, then I would treat no one differently. Would you all want to be the same? If I made one person tall and another short, then this would give some advantages to the taller person in some situations, and advantages to the short person in other situations.

Life is to be lived for what it is. I would like you to explore the riches that life can offer, but it will remain imperfect. This very imperfection is a source of many of the joys of life – a good day is so much sweeter when it has followed a bad day.

This response solicited a follow up question by the German delegate.

"Like my Japanese colleague, until today, I was not convinced of the existence of God. I like to think that I was fairer of mind in my agnostic stance, but it was probably more the case that I was hedging my bets."

"The single thing that turned me away from religions was the contradiction between claims that you are all loving, all compassionate and all powerful, and yet are able to allow such suffering to permeate the lives of so many people."

"Being held hostage, as it were, by Satan, I can understand why such suffering might have persisted. And I have indeed noticed in the last few weeks some strange changes in the world. Amongst other unusual events, an interim report from a seismology conference in Japan claims that tectonic plate collision activity has all but ceased. I strongly believe that you were responsible for this sudden change. The report even speculated this, although at the time I dismissed this as a foolish whim."

"My question to you is this. Do you plan to remove all suffering from the world?" he asked of the Lord.

And the Lord replied :

You ask a very good question. Whilst held hostage, as you say, I was often aware of the degree of suffering that beset the world and its people and animals. And yes, I do of course care equally for all of my creatures.

It grieved me deeply that I was witness to so much pain and suffering in the world, whilst being incapable of doing enough about it. My plan now is to carry out a Balancing Act – to redress the greater imbalances in the world.

Suffering has its rightful place in the world – it is right that you have toothache when your tooth needs repairing because you ate too much sweet food. But this toothache will no longer keep you awake at night. And those that eat sensibly – those that have their own

lives in balance – will not suffer thus. I will ensure such fairness, as I abhor unnecessary pain and suffering.

However, they are still a part of the fabric of life. But if there is too much, then life is pushed to one side. If your life is so heavily impacted by suffering, then you are not living a full life.

I want to give you equality – so that each of you can have a broadly equal capacity to live a full life. Every life itself will be different, but I will remove arbitrary and pointless suffering, from insomnia to cancer. However, this subject is too large to discuss fully now.

Can I please have the next question?

The Baha'I faith representative was next …

"With the advent of the Internet, there is a huge clash of theist and non theist argument concerning the origin of life on Earth. The atheists and scientists declare evolution as the answer to all such questions, furnished as it is with a wealth of evidence. The theists counter argue with Intelligent Design. Can you please enlighten us all?" he asked.

God answered this somewhat tricky question :

I am supposed to have created all life on the planet. This, I assure you, is both true and false. Evolution theory describes well the changes in each species on earth as time passes. But it describes change, not instigation. The creation of life from non life in the first place is called Abiogenesis. This is where I was involved. I live outside of the domain of the Earth much as a human resides outside of a fish tank.

When I created the first simple organisms, I was not aware that life would evolve into such complex creatures as humans. But you are my ultimate creation, and I care for you, much as a good Mother cares for her son whether he grows up to be good or bad.

I have the power to manipulate matter on Earth in ways that you would not understand. But life is fragile, and the joy of the diversity of your lives becomes the joy of my life. Likewise, when you suffer, I suffer.

If you want to ascribe the creation of life as it is now to anyone, you should give the credit to cells. You were created by cell division and specialisation. I claim credit for creating the first simple uni-cellular and simple multi-cellular organisms, and steering subsequent evolution.

As my powers were being weakened by those satanic forces, the interplay of life-forms took many bad paths that I could no longer fix.

Now I am able to start remedying the problems that lead to so much suffering in the world.

And so the questions continued. God patiently explained that killing in the name of God, by whatever name, was fundamentally unsociable, and thereby not desirable.

He explained that He was only capable of part of this great Balancing Act. He explained that the growing divide between the very rich and very poor was of no real health or happiness benefit for the rich or of course for the poor – the rich were way richer than they needed to be, rarely gaining from their excesses, and often suffering from the imbalance they it created in their lives.

God fielded questions for a further two hours, after which he concluded this extraordinary programme :

I will leave you now, for I have much to do elsewhere.

I thank you for listening to me, and for your questions.

I look forward to a more harmonious world as the years pass.

Please go in peace.

Mental Gravities
The gravity of habit and other forces

I want to highlight to you how pervasive and persuasive mental gravities are in our lives, and thereby help you to start releasing yourself them from their pull. We are all physically drawn to the earth by its gravity, but our minds and thoughts are drawn by mental equivalents. Many of these mental gravities do not serve us well. At the same time, we are mostly unaware of them. They operate below our conscious radar.

We are held by the gravity of **habit**, where we automatically, unconsciously repeat former behaviours. We are likewise bound to use and defend **knowledge** we have gathered over the years, again often not fully aware that we are doing so unthinkingly.

Both of these automatic deferrals to what we have acquired illustrates how our brains likes to conserve energy. (Even so, the brain is still very greedy on body fuel for its size). Consequential to this economy are shortcuts and shallowness of thinking.

Rules that we feel obliged to follow can also assert a mental pull to the point where we can fall into the trap of blindly following them and thereby concluding that 'this is just how things are'. Often referred to as *path dependence*, it is where we can lose sight of *why* the rule was instigated in the first place.

Even something as simple as the **form** and **function** of something can exert a gravitational pull. Someone had the innovative idea of making a base for an electric kettle so that filling it up no longer required the mains lead to be unplugged. The kettle sat on an abbreviated form of the plug. But the gravity of 'plugging in' was retained. So the shape of the plug on the base was the same as the lead plug, requiring precise kettle alignment. It was redesigned to be circular in shape, allowing easy seating of the kettle.

The famous football manager Louis Van Gaal declared that football is a game principally played using your feet, so when the ball goes into touch on the side of the pitch, a 'throw-in' was a silly idea. Much better to have a free kick, not least because throw-ins often concede possession back to their opponent. Here, he was challenging rules, of course. The dogma of what sticks 'because that is how it has always been' is so powerful for most of us that we stop even thinking about questioning rules. We are trapped in their gravitational pull. Established familiarity gives the rules a 'correctness'.

Having played hundreds of ad-hoc, bags-for-posts games of football in a large park nearby, I have a full-range of experience of team sizes. On one occasion, I played an hour of 2-a-side. Not to be recommended as it is ludicrously tiring as well as not particularly entertaining for any spectators who might happen to be watching. At the other extreme, influxes of late arrivers have resulted in games in excess of 20-a-side. With so little possession time for each player, it is also not to be recommended for playing or watching. At the lower end of the scale, but accepted as a valid team size, 5-a-side games can be fast and furious and exciting to play in. But they lack the expansive majesty of a full-sized game, goals and pitch.

So what is the 'optimum' size team for a game? From my perspective, around about 8 outfield players makes for the best games. This is an opinion, of course, but one derived from the experience of all those many games of varying team sizes. Curiously enough, the size of the pitch for such games is less critical to the game than the number of players, although 8-a-side on a full-sized 11-a-side pitch might be too demanding.

So why do football games have 10 outfield players? It is extremely likely that it was chosen as a nice round number. Yes, it really could be as simple as that. When the game was in its fledgling state, there would not have been too much concern or experience casting doubt on that number. And since it works pretty well, as is evident, it suck. Then, crucially, it gained momentum. The longer something is established, the more it is accepted. The weight of experience bears more heavily than the validity or appropriateness of the original decision.

However, football with 10 outfield players has, of course, been gigantically successful. But a matter that justifies a challenge to team size is that there are generally very few goals in games, even after 90 minutes. With 8 outfield players there would undoubtably be more goals, courtesy of less defensive armoury. This is evident even now in 11-a-side games, when a team breaks from defence to launch a counter-attack against a much depleted opponent defence. But you get my point, hopefully, to start challenging the **status quo**. The assumption that the rules were wise is not always valid.

To show how far we can go when challenging 'how things are', I want to discuss a football matter that baffles and infuriates in near equal measure. The *offside rule*. It was introduced early in the game to stop players 'goal-hanging'. Teams would leave some strikers near the opposing goal and hoof the ball towards them for easy goal-scoring opportunities. A mechanism was needed to stop this. So the off-side rule was born, initially demanding that there were at least 2 defenders and goalkeeper ahead of an opposing player when he received the ball. If he was further ahead, a free-kick would be given for transgressing the rule.

Later the, rule was relaxed to reduce it to 1 defender and goalkeeper. Player A below is therefore off-side at the moment now that player B in his team is passing the ball to him :

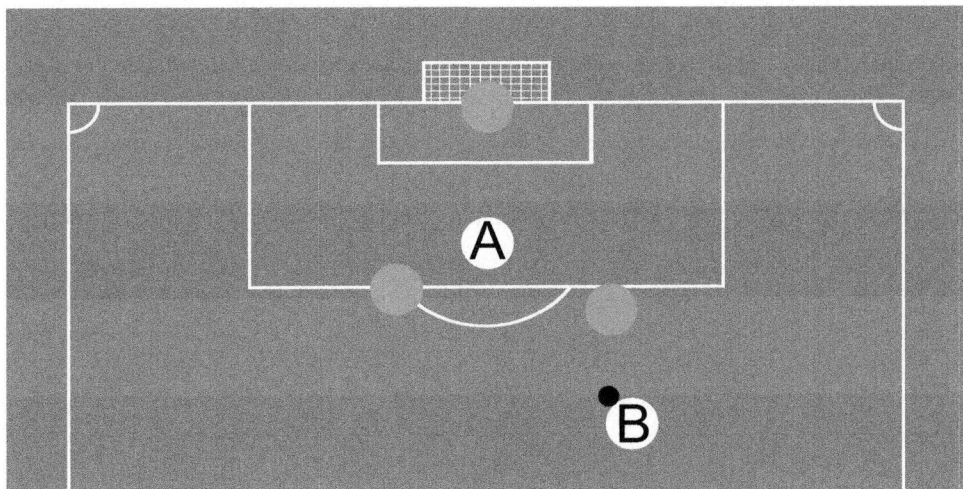

Notice that he is slightly ahead of the last defender. The rule is regulated by a linesman who tries to stay at the same level as that last defender. He imagines a straight line across the pitch that is at the very front of that defender. If he glimpses a striker ahead of that line, he whistles off-side.

What I have described encapsulates the concept of off-side in a manageable way. It is a *proxy* for the spirit of the reason for the off-side concept that seeks to stop a player goal-hanging. You can see that it is a *limited* approximation of what is needed in the image below, where A is the same far advanced but off to the left of the pitch :

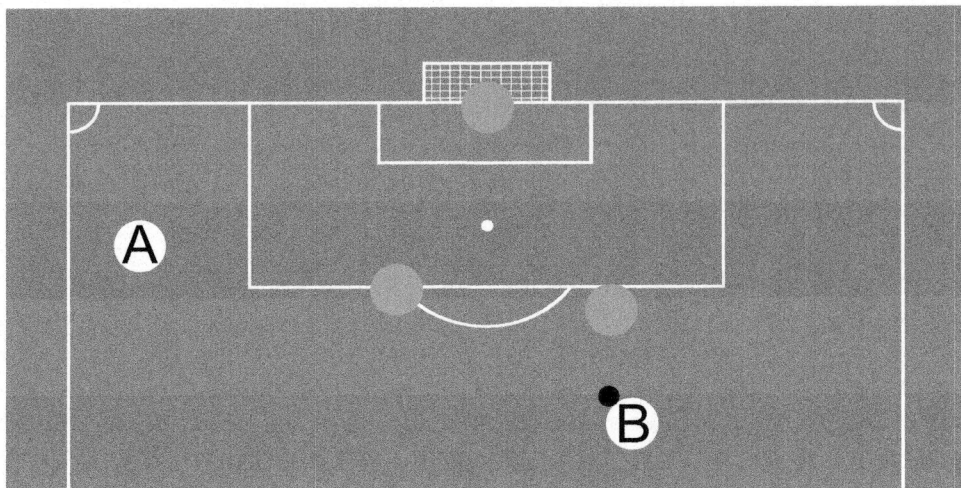

Player A would be treated as off-side, yet is clearly not goal-hanging. He is most certainly much further away from the goal than that last defender. The spirit of stopping goal-hanging is being missed by the simplified nature of the measurement deployed.

I will digress now and return to this point. Bear with me. When a penalty is being taken, all players must be outside the penalty area – the 18 yard box – to avoid interference with the penalty. But immediately behind the penalty spot, players would be very close to the penalty taker. So an extension to the penalty area is added to maintain a 10 yard distance by all players. It is the 'D' curve, or penalty arc :

I mention this curve because a curve rather than a straight line would deliver a more accurate, spirit-aligned measurement of off-side that would then more correctly find the player on the far left touchline as *on-side*.

But that would mean many curved lines radiating out from the goal, as the last defender position down the pitch necessarily varies, unlike the penalty spot. So to measure off-side in the spirit of the law is highly impractical.

The short-comings of the straight line measurement are being exposed by VAR, the Video Assistant Referee and technology that now awards off-side to players far more precisely than lines-men can do. A player was recently off-side by about 1 inch. The game commentators were up in arms! But it was a correct call according to the rules.

However, it not only exposed the limitations of the straight line measure (the player was indeed actually further away from goal than the last defender), but also a lack of common sense in the measure. Why oh why did they not treat a player off-side *only* when there is a clear gap between them and the last defender? That would have a much greater chance of being more in the spirit of the game. To give the striker the benefit of latitude since goals are the life-blood of the game. Many supporters of the notion that off-side is off-side no matter how marginal are pulled by the *gravity* of the implementation of the rule, and miss the *spirit* and reason of the rule.

One of the consequences of the momentum of the status quo – that 'this is how things have always been' – is that we can get saddled with such compromises. But the more established a rule, behaviour or system, the more people are frightened of challenging it, and the more vilified they are for trying to do so. Ozan Varol's marvellous book "Think like a rocket scientist" was largely influential on the thinking and motivation behind this article. He describes a plethora of innovation and design ideas, and the methods that many innovators use to release themselves from the gravity of current thinking and mindsets. He shows how persistent some design 'choices' can be, unchallenged yet ripe for challenge :

> *The width of the engines that powered the space shuttle – one of the most complex machines humankind has ever created – was determined over two thousand years ago by a Roman road engineer. Yes, you read that correctly.*
>
> *The engines were 4 feet 8.5 inches wide because that was the width of the rail line that would carry them from Utah to Florida.*
>
> *The width of that rail line in turn, was based on the width of tramlines in England.*
>
> *The width of the tramlines, in turn, was based on the width of the roads built by the Romans. 4 feet 8.5 inches.*

Sometimes, even the label or name given to something can exert a gravitational pull. The welfare system in Britain was conceived as a social safety net, providing financial and other support in times of need. But political ideology saw financial payments as 'something for nothing', so renamed it from 'social security' to 'benefits'. Clearly, the new name is at least partly correct – recipients are indeed benefitting from state aid. But it reframed the payments as a *gain above need*. Recipients could now be seen to be state 'scroungers'. The weight of the word is immense. The state payment is the same, but the label has a large gravitational pull, making some recipients feel guilty.

By way of another financial example, the word 'tax' has a burdensome, 'taxing' gravity. It has acquired a punitive feel, the focus placed almost exclusively on the payment of tax, along with a culture that actually normalises the notion of minimising, avoiding or evading tax. The other side of the equation is only readily felt when we release our minds from the gravity or gravitas of paying our dues. We can then see the purpose of tax as essentially a 'civilised society contribution', paying for healthcare, education, prisons, roads etc., and of course welfare systems. The excess wealth of the fortunate helps to support the unfortunate.

Our education system is responsible for many mental gravities, some of which really do not serve us well. A very fundamental gravity is the curriculum. It is so central, so sacrosanct in most education systems, that the rounded, multi-faceted development of children is largely compromised. One casualty of the largely academic nature of most curricula is play and playfulness. It is permitted in short bursts during lesson breaks, sidelined to the periphery. In Finland, however, play is central to child development, with formal education not starting until about age 7. However, education through play is present, even if the curriculum setters elsewhere are too drawn by the gravity of importance of their academic lessons to embrace that concept. Curriculum-based education is largely a quantified, organised, testable education methodology. Learning through play is seen as a dangerous undermining of those 'desirables'. But sustaining and enhancing the playful, creative and sociable aspects of a child's development is vital in a world where innovative thinking is highly prized. Innovation requires a mindset that is released from the gravity of 'how things are' :

> *"Playfulness is a deliberate, temporary relaxation of rules in order to explore the possibilities of alternative rules"*
>
> *James March*
>
> *"We are drowning in information, while starving for wisdom."*
>
> *E. O. Wilson*

One of the drivers of creativity is actually a surprise. Boredom. Yet the gravitational pull of electronic devices and a life-style that keeps us permanently busy misjudges boredom. It fails also to see that sitting doing nothing – becoming a human *being* again instead of a human *doing* – is not a waste of time. The *doing nothing* label has a great pull on us. It can make us feel guilty just sitting in a state of calm.

I think I can convince you of the value of a time empty of our normal 'doing life' activities. In 1990, a lady was stuck at a railway station, awaiting a train that was delayed by no less than 4 hours. It allowed her to revisit an idea for a book she had, at a time when there were no mobile phones to absorb her attention. By the time the train arrived, she had fully fleshed out the story she wanted to write. Her name was J.K.Rowling, and thus was born the first Harry Potter book!

Another constraining effect of the nature of most modern education systems is the conditioning of young minds. Not just the suppression or sidelining of creative and challenging thinking, but the training of thinking in predetermined ways. This conditioning becomes a massive gravitational force in life. It demands that we think this is how things are and such acquired thinking, rules and knowledge are *de facto* correct and beyond challenge. The minds of children are steered along the same paths, denying difference amongst them.

The rather splendid German word *Einstellung* describes one of the outcomes of this conditioning :

> *Einstellung is the development of a mechanised state of mind. Often called a problem solving set, Einstellung refers to a person's predisposition to solve a given problem in a specific manner even though better or more appropriate methods of solving the problem exist.*
>
> *Wikipedia*

Except that this is not really what Einstellung means. A German friend was puzzled at its use in psychology parlance since it essentially means **attitude** in German. But name aside, the effect described is a consequence of the gravity of mindset that rote teaching can create.

Most especially in mathematics, we are given clearly defined problems specifically chosen to exercise one and only one mathematical technique, with one and only one answer :

> *The students take the pre-packaged and pre-approved problem and plug it into a formula they memorised, which in turn spits out the right answer.*
>
> *Ozan Voral*

An encapsulated, idealised situation that bears little relationship with the real world, where we have to recognise the problem ourselves, determine the constraints and concepts and work out which mathematical techniques might be deployed to solve the problem. We are actually conditioned into *not* challenging the teacher as authority figure *nor* in challenging the problems they set us, *nor* challenging the demands they place on us to stick to the rules. We are taught a gravity-creating importance of 'doing things this way and only this way'. If a child finds a creative way of solving the problem, but happens to make a calculation error, it is rare that the creative path taken will be explored. It would likely be invalidated immediately as it yielded the wrong answer. The gravity of 'getting the right answer' largely kills the creative path.

And the atomisation of mathematical techniques into discrete, unconnected lessons is also a poor reflection of the real world. The tools are offered but not the context for their use. Teaching works better when the real world is the starting point. To teach some mathematics and mechanics, for example, by working out how wheelbarrows work. How far one revolution of the wheel will take it. How the forces to keep it upright operate. Such real-world teaching brings these subjects alive.

Tests and exams are powerful drivers of education systems. Their undoubted importance makes them uber-powerful gravitational forces, so much so that they are actually allowed to pervert the education system.

First perversion is the 'teaching to the test' problem, where the gravity of the tests themselves feedbacks into the lessons so that absorption of facts often displaces understanding. Where revision sessions are deemed vital, yet are a declaration that the lessons were not absorbed properly in the first place. Where performance in tests becomes a focus, an obsession. Yet tests should be means of feedback to children to find shortcomings in order to help them improve upon those shortcomings.

Second is the focus of teaching on matters that are *quantifiable* and *measurable*. In particular, and a personal matter of great frustration, is the intense focus on grammar when learning English. I struggled immensely with the nature of the archaic terminology, with its awkwardness and with my acute inability to remember the terms. This focus on the quantifiable and testable attends to the tools of the language, much as formulae are the tools of mathematics. But language is a vehicle to communicate and entertain. What is is easy to test – the grammar – misses the big picture in order to avoid the *qualifiable* matter of prose and succinctness and picture painting and story telling. And the verbalisation or oration of these. This is what language should be about.

Third is the defining of the value and nature of a child by their test and exam results. A single metric or grade per subject! I received an E grade in my Art 'A' level exam here in Wales in large part because the painting and history-of-art essays I submitted were of poor quality. Yet I am a fine pencil-drawing artist, receiving paid commissions after leaving school. Children are not their grades. They are so much more. A great orator but poor writer will receive a poor English language grade. A child excelling at social skills will not be measured on, or valued by those skills.

The gravitational force of conditioned thinking from education systems continues, of course, into life. When situations would benefit from lateral thinking, few of us are practiced in this art. I became frustrated with the rather stiff controls of my shiny new microwave oven. They became impossibly hard to turn when my fingers were wet. Of course, when buying the microwave, the gravity of appearance and basic functionality pushed other considerations away. It never occurred to me to actually even try to turn the controls. I felt the force of 'this is how things are' for a long while. So I put up with this irritating problem. For months!

Then I decided to fix it. Am I allowed to enhance this device? Warranty may be invalidated if I did. But I decided that the problem was too bad to ignore. I wanted a tactile surface to grab. So the linear thinking that school conditions was operating with me, even though I like to be creative. So I was looking to use double sided tape wrapped around each control with thin rubber laid on top from some gloves I would cut up to do the job.

This too was linear, conditioned thinking. The problem was influencing the solution too much. I broke this thinking by realising that some rubber bands would do the trick. Two minutes later is was sorted :

Knowledge and expertise can become gravitational forces. We become very biassed into favouring what we know and understand, and limit ourselves, often rejecting contrary or competing notions. The sponge-like nature of the young mind sadly often becomes calcified, leading to this wonderful paradox :

> *In the beginner's mind, there are many possibilities.*
>
> *In the expert's mind there are few.*
>
> Shunryu Susuki

The history of science is littered with proponents of accepted theories that hung to those theories for dear life while they were being debunked. The gravity of the reputation that the theory gained them, and their investment in it served to make them behave that way.

If you have a rare of relatively unique medical condition, it is actually better to seek consultation with a junior medical practitioner. An expert is more likely to match your symptoms with what he knows. That knowledge will exert a pull that often blinds them to the nuances that a less experienced consultant might more likely see. The expert often wants to use his knowledge, and not abandon it for something new that puts them on the same footing as a novice!

A cleverly conceived chess problem was given to some expert and amateur chess players, where a sequence of moves that would lead to check-mate in 5 moves. A standard, conventional series of moves. However, there was also a mate in 3 moves that required unusual move choices. The experts all found the 5 move sequence. But amateurs were more likely to find the 3 move sequence. They actually observed the eye movements of the experts and discovered that they kept playing through the standard moves that they were thoroughly used to playing. They were trapped in the gravity of correct technique when unusual, quirky play revealed a better result.

Sven Magnus Øen Carlsen is the World Chess Champion at the time of writing. In 2013, he was challenger to the then World Champion, Viswanathan Anand, a player renowned for a computer-like memory for openings and tactics. A master, but bound by knowledge. Carlsen, by contrast, is characterised by creativity, unbound by expertise, able to innovate on the fly. He confounded his opponent by moving him outside the precise bounds of his knowledge. Arnand was forced to think almost as a novice. And he mostly floundered, conceding his title.

Since then, Carlsen has remained World Chess Champion for 7 years, doing so by varying his opening moves to confound those who prepare for matches with him.

In light of that release for the grip of knowledge, the world chess champions are in unison with this wisdom :

> *When you see a good move, do not make it immediately. Look for a better one.*

I appear to have omitted a very significant mental gravity so far. One that increasingly pervades our modern lives. Short-term thinking is damaging the balance in our individual lives and in National economies and businesses. Indigenous species existed for millennia in balance with their environment as they traded short-term greed for long-term thinking. Sadly, we clamour for ever more instant gratification, ignoring or blinding ourselves to the long term consequences.

This focus on immediacy of outcome can also blind us to the path to the outcome. When we learn how to play a top-spin backhand in tennis we all too easily treat success as the ball spinning fast to the other side of the net, and inside the lines. We are getting it all back to front. We should focus on the *technique* regardless of the subsequent flight of the ball or where the ball lands. Getting the technique right will eventually lead to the outcome we seek. We have to suffer failure of outcome while learning. We only do that by releasing ourselves from the gravity of instant reward.

In much the same way, a rugby team should focus on individual and team skills and coordination rather than on winning matches. Winning with bad technique make work short term, but is no recipe for long term success.

Governments largely operate with policies that secure a repeat term in office –they are virtually obliged by fixed terms to do so. A focus on looking good in the short term.

The culture in business and economics education, of focussing on competition and profit tends to carry through into business and corporation behaviours. The sense that they must compete with whatever it takes to survive in the short-term in a dog-eat-dog culture. This is especially true when corporations are generally obliged to furnish an endless series of quarterly dividends to their shareholders. That these shareholders *expect* such dividends, and therefore often demand them, adds to the intense focus on short-term gain.

The gravitational pull of profit is like the tail wagging the dog. A business or corporation should exist to provide products and/or services to customers, yet all too often, they exist to extract maximal profit from their customers. It creates perversions, for example where business- rather than state-operated prisons are incentivised to ramp up the number of members of public they incarcerate. And to retain them for as long as possible.

The greatest victim of the gravity of private profit acquisition is the planet. Resources are extracted for free since economists and governments were too glibly happy to hide that imbalance of accountability. Likewise the use of the environment as a free dumping ground for waste.

The gravitas of this short-term mental gravity is the greatest of all, likely to bring an end to our species.

Go

The board game that the West ignores ...
... yet it is much older & richer than Chess

Originating in China somewhere between 2,500 and 4,000 years ago, the board game called Go has mesmerised and intrigued in a way that Chess in the West never quite has.

Edward Lasker said of Go :

"The rules of Go are so elegant, organic and rigorously logical that if intelligent life forms exist elsewhere in the universe they almost certainly play go."

These are the words of an International Chess Master, so deep was the effect of the game upon him. Wars have been decided by a game between leaders. The game company Atari was chosen by one of the directors after a move in the game. This Japanese term loosely means 'hit, success, reaching the mark'. Whilst Go started in China, it was adopted as the National game of Japan around the 7th century CE, determining the terminology language.

The board shown on the previous page is called a *GoBan*. The top end GoBans are made from a single section of wood from the Kaya tree. This tree is chosen because of the quality of resonant sound it solicits when a stone is placed down onto the board. The Japanese place aesthetics high in their sensibilities.

It was so much a part of Japanese culture that it become one of the arts, along with poetry and calligraphy that young ladies learnt :

Whilst mass market 'stones' are made of plastic or glass, the best quality stones are in a different league.

The White stones are carved from clamshell, and the Black stones from slate.

Shiny White and matt Black.

Professional Go flourishes across Japan, Korea and China, with matches shown live on TV with millions of viewers.

A Japanese anime TV and book series promoted the game to the young, reigniting passion in the game :

The rules of Go are very simple, in many ways more so than Chess. However, much like Chess, Go is a hugely engrossing game of great elegance and astonishing depth and richness. It will handsomely reward your efforts in learning the game.

One of the beauties of Go is that it is also a forgiving game. There have been many occasions where I have played a disastrous opening yet been able to recover and easily win. In Chess, recovery from a major setback is not nearly so common.

As you learn Go, you also acquire habits that transfer very well to life itself. With greater experience, you learn not to put all your eggs in one basket, to not chase lost causes, and no longer weep over the spilling of milk, as it were. It may take you a fair few games to get the feel of Go, but the game will gradually start to reveal its beauty. I still play most days against players all around the World, via the Internet, my love for the game untarnished since I was given my first Go set by my brother in 1990.

Here is a view looking down onto a Go board from above. This is a full sized board, with 19 vertical and 19 horizontal lines :

Notice that it is slightly taller than it is wide. This makes the board look square when you sit in front of it. Beginner boards have either 9 by 9 or 13 by 13 sets of lines.

Whilst Go can be scaled to any sized board, 19 by 19 was eventually adopted as providing the best quality game. And 19 by 19 is the size used for the vast majority of games played today.

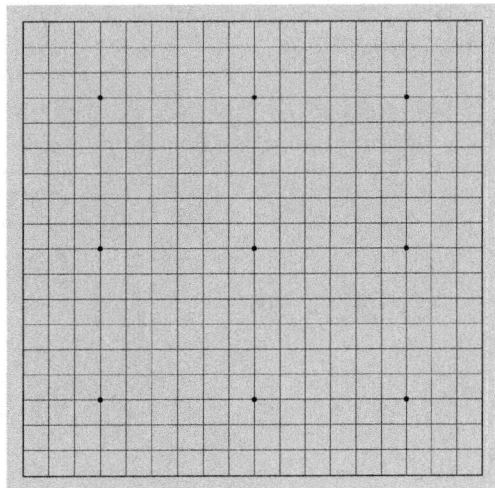

73

Go is a game of territory – you battle to surround more of the board than your opponent. This campaign for territory often results in many local boundary fights, so that Go is more like a war than the single battle to capture the opposing King in Chess. Just as battles get lost and won in a real War, individual losses and gains in a game of Go do not dictate the overall outcome, but influence the way the game evolves.

Unlike Chess, Go is played on the intersections of these lines. When you play your first move, you have a choice of 361 (19 x 19) intersections to play on.

The little black dots have two purposes. First, to make it easy to make moves in ideal positions in the corners – tried and tested opening moves. Secondly, as handicap positions – if you are weaker than your opponent, you get to place stones on some or all of these handicap points before your opponent plays their first move. (Japanese rules are used in this book – in Chinese rules, handicap stones can be placed freely).

The player with the Black stones starts the game by playing a stone on any of the empty intersections. White then plays a stone on another empty intersection. They continue taking turns to place stones on empty intersections. As they proceed, the board gradually fills with stones.

I will show the basic rules of how to play Go using a beginner's 9 by 9 board just to keep things nice and simple. In keeping with convention, I will show just the playing lines – not the border around the board. Note that there is nothing special about the thickness of the outer lines.

What do I mean when I say that Go is a territorial game? Imagine that the board is an island with sea all around. The 81 intersections – we call them points – is the starting territory. To own a part of this territory, you must build a wall of stones that surround that part.

So you start with empty, uncharted land and take turns to try to grab a bigger share of that land than your opponent. That is how you win.

A starting move :

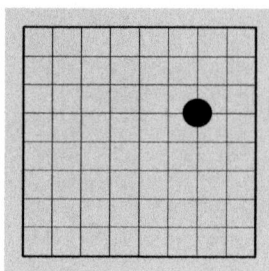

Unlike Chess, note that the stone does not sit on a square but sits on an intersection of two lines. The lines show connections between adjacent stones.

As sole occupier of the land, Black currently owns **all** of the remaining 80 empty points. Like Chess, each player takes turns to place stones on the board. They keep doing so until nothing more can be gained by playing any more stones. Here is the White reply :

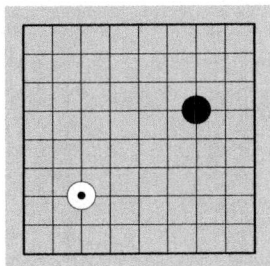

I put a dot in the middle of the last stone placed on the board. Now that he has competition, Black is no longer the sole owner of the land. He shares it with White. As it stands, neither player has completely surrounded any empty points. So they need to add more stones to start making walls around territory. Black may therefore have a plan to place stones along the marked line below :

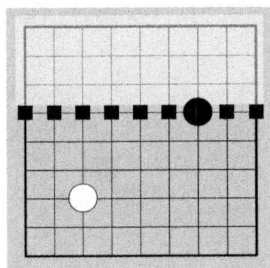

If he were able to complete it, he would own the marked empty points above. That would be a full 9 x 3 = 27 points of profit (remember that the edge of the board needs no defence). Of course, White may not want Black to complete his plan ... but Black starts to enact his plan, playing carefully like this :

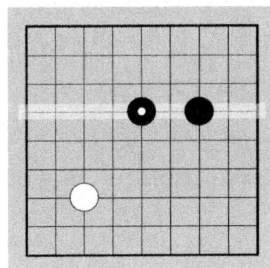

He has made a one-space extension from his stone to start building that wall. He sensibly spaces out his stones, realising that playing one point at a time would be too slow.

But White can still immediately disrupt the Black plan ...

If White does not respond to this atari, Black can capture it. Unlike chess, losing pieces is rarely fatal, so the game offers much greater scope for recovery after loss :

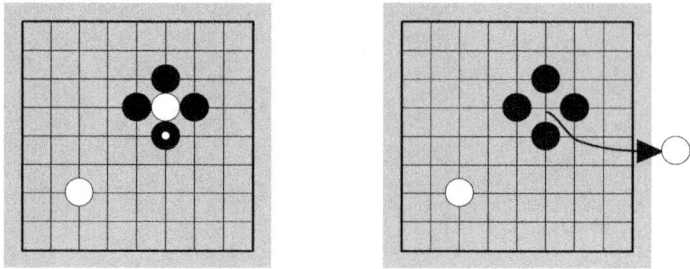

A stone or a chain of stones that has had its last liberty removed is captured and removed from the board. Captured stones – prisoners – add to the territory count for a player.

Beginners get obsessed about capturing or saving from capture. But good Go is richer than just this. White could have avoided or delayed capture by adding a stone to the one in atari:

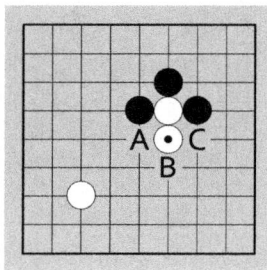

By adding one stone, White creates a 2 stone **chain** with 3 liberties at A, B and C. If Black wants to capture this White chain, he requires 3 moves now! Stones that form a connected chain like the White stones, or are close together like the Black stones are called **groups**.

It is important to point out that the 2 stone White group is no longer an easy target for Black. If he wanted to capture, he would have to play three moves *without reply* to do so :

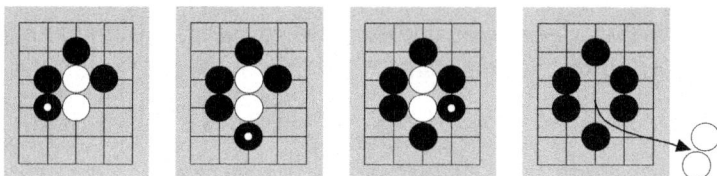

If White does not respond to this atari, Black can capture it. Unlike chess, losing pieces is rarely fatal, so the game offers much greater scope for recovery after loss :

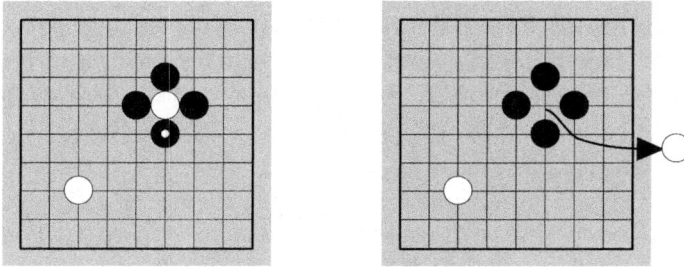

A stone or a chain of stones that has had its last liberty removed is captured and removed from the board. Captured stones – prisoners – add to the territory count for a player.

Beginners get obsessed about capturing or saving from capture. But good Go is richer than just this. White could have avoided or delayed capture by adding a stone to the one in atari:

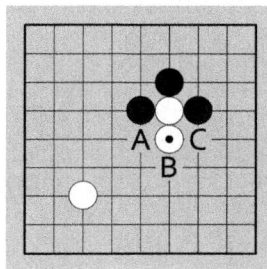

By adding one stone, White creates a 2 stone **chain** with 3 liberties at A, B and C. If Black wants to capture this White chain, he requires 3 moves now! Stones that form a connected chain like the White stones, or are close together like the Black stones are called **groups**.

It is important to point out that the 2 stone White group is no longer an easy target for Black. If he wanted to capture, he would have to play three moves *without reply* to do so :

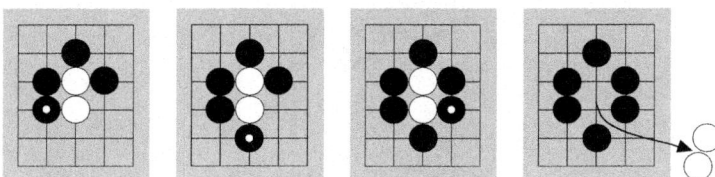

White would probably defend before all 3 moves were made. White might even let Black capture since it would allow White to play 3 moves elsewhere and gain more than he loses.

Many books teaching newcomers Go focus heavily on capture as the starting point. Instead, I focus on the whole board – the acquisition of territory – with fighting an incidental part. In actual games, fighting does become very important, but beginners taught 'capture Go' can get obsessed by capturing and lose whole board balance.

Because it takes 3 moves to capture, it can be unwise to keep chasing it senselessly. You will see shortly that Black can actually resume construction of his wall instead. When capturing on the edge of the board, that edge acts as a surround :

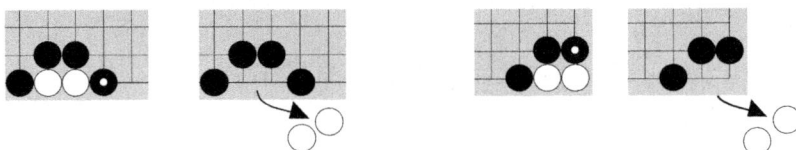

If we look at the game now, we can see the effect of the White move and how Black continues with his wall :

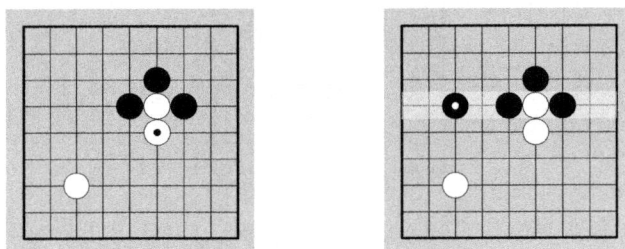

Now you can see Black getting much closer to his aim of securing territory. And White is lagging behind – his stones do not yet form a wall around land. The White attack had in effect helped strengthen Black to an extent.

But all is not lost for White. He has created a kink in the Black wall that he can exploit:

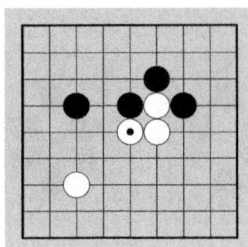

At this point, you may be wondering why I am showing you a game in progress. As if I had forgotten to tell you all the rules. The point is that the basic rules in Go are very simple. You can already play Go from what you have learnt so far. Unlike Chess, where there are different movements for each stone, Go is purer – homogenous in effect – where each stone has the same attributes.

There are some more concepts to explain, but I'll bring them up as a natural part of this game rather than describe them as abstractions. The Black wall is under attack, so he defends safely and solidly :

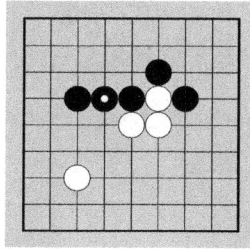

White can press again on the other side :

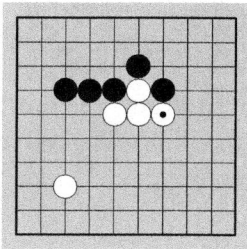

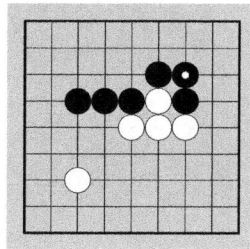

This example game shows some typical small board play. The game is quite close, but Black may win as his position is more solid – there are no weaknesses in his shape.

So far, play has been divided in two. It is often more messy than that, especially on a full sized board. After White fixes a weakness as a way of trying to secure more of the board than Black has, then Black jumps right inside the 'White area':

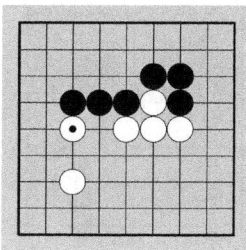

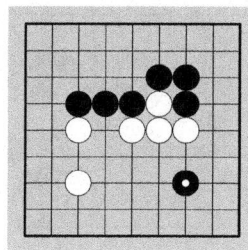

You see the Black mini-moyo taking shape now.

It is not yet a fully sealed or complete area. It is more like a framework, called a **moyo** in Japanese. When invading here, Black is looking to make a miniature moyo in the corner, thereby neutralising most of the White moyo. If he succeeds, he wins the game easily. White starts by squeezing Black into a small area :

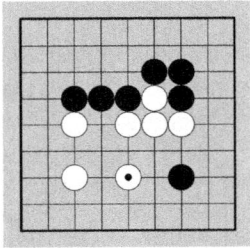

He tries to connect to his upper side stones, but White can easily block him :

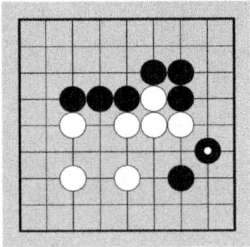

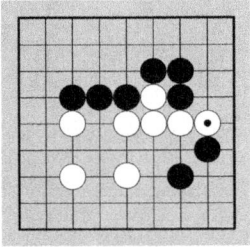

Black is slowly being squeezed into the corner by White. He must try to make a miniature moyo in the corner. A moyo within what was a White moyo – like Russian dolls. Black starts to create that corner moyo :

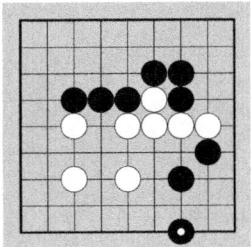

White looks to cut into it with a 'peep' move :

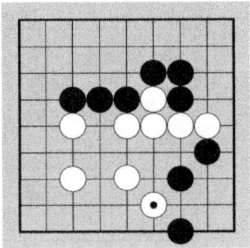

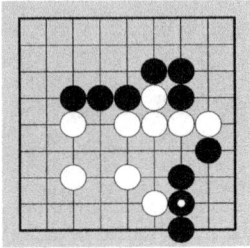

You see the Black mini-moyo taking shape now.

80

White now squeezes further, threatening to play an atari at A to capture the marked stone :

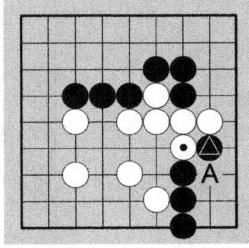

So Black makes more corner space by extending, and White matches :

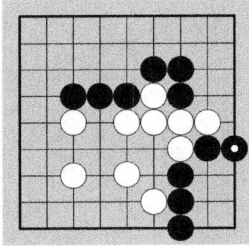

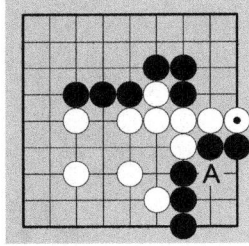

The two Black stones again have only 2 liberties. So White now threatens to atari and eat them by playing at A.

Black defends indirectly :

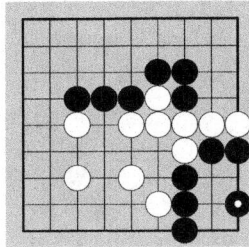

Now, if White plays the atari, his stone itself is now put into atari when Black defends :

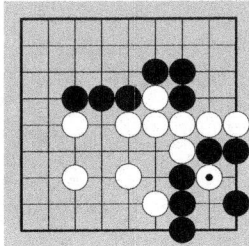

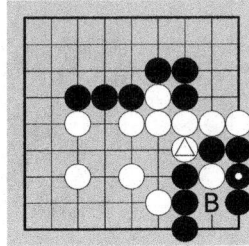

The White stone only has one liberty at B. It is vital to note that the White stone is **not** diagonally connected to the marked stone – stones are only connected into chains via direct horizontal or vertical contact. Rather than White killing Black stones, Black has grown so strong that he is ready to eat a White stone.

81

White can try to escape by extending since it does put the Black chain of stones into atari, but the White chain remains in atari and Black now captures them :

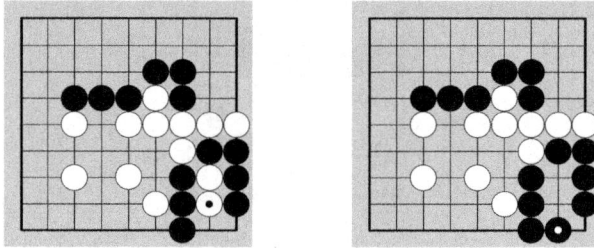

And now Black has a shape that cannot be captured by White. Even if White tries to wrap around it, he cannot kill these Black corner stones, as you will soon see:

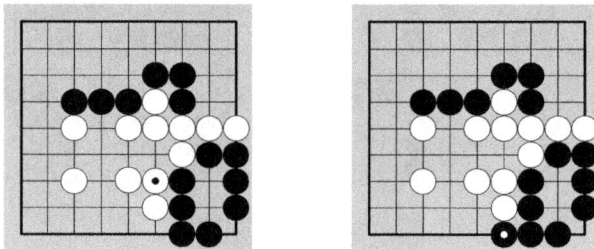

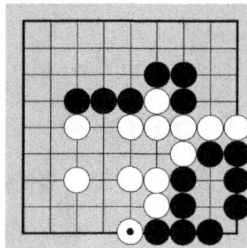

It is Black's move now. We'll get him to start shoring up the upper side moyo, and then see if White can start to surround the Black corner stones – from the inside!

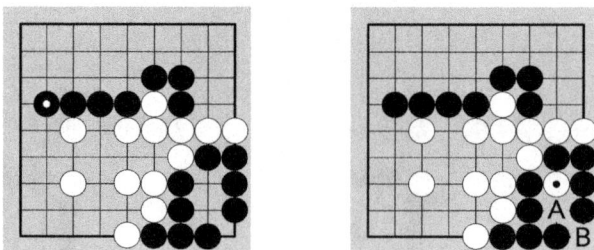

White goes inside. But what next? He is immediately in atari. Black can take next move. Except that he does not have to because White has not placed any Black stones in atari. And White cannot extend to A as this would be suicide, losing all his liberties *without killing* anything. Playing at B would also be suicide, which is illegal in Go. Black is alive with two 'eyes' as the terminology goes. It surrounds two *separate* empty areas – White cannot simultaneously play in both to completely surround Black.

Black does not get many points, but by living here, he takes away half of the White moyo. White has lost the game because Black already surrounds more territory than Black. And White cannot catch up.

I have played some finishing moves to get to the game completion here :

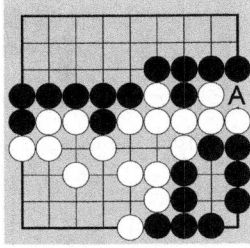

The winner in a game of Go is the player with the most points surrounded, with prisoner stones captured adding to the tally. The point A on the right is neutral – neither player surrounds this exclusively.

Black has 23 points on the upper side and 3 points in the corner, while White has 14 points. So Black wins by 12 points, although White is often given a **komi** bonus for starting second in the game.

In a full 19 by 19 point board, komi is normally 5.5 points. The half point is added to avoid a drawn game.

What if White played differently in the corner? If he stopped Black making two eyes and living, the result of the game would be very different.

So White plays here instead of at A :

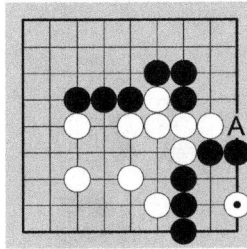

There is a way for Black to still live in the corner. But let's show a way that does not work :

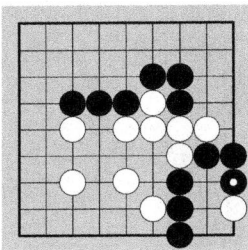

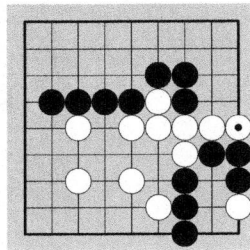

White puts Black in atari before Black can put the White stone in atari. So Black must defend :

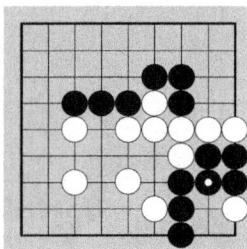

White must now stop Black creating two eyes :

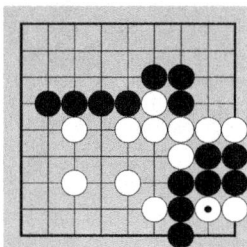

Black can now place these two stones in atari, but will not get the two eyes needed :

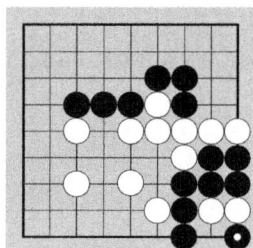

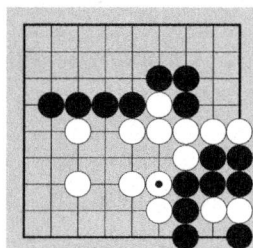

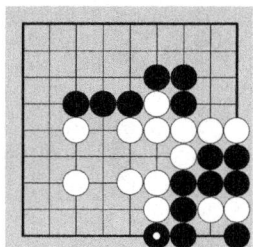

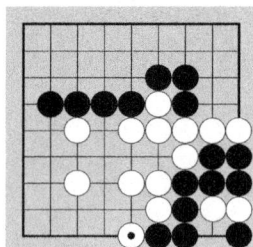

White has now put Black in atari. When he takes he is reduced to a single eye :

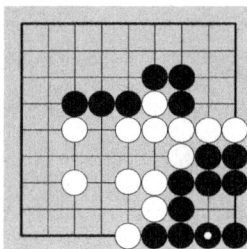

White does not need to kill. The group is dead already. A dead group of stone does not have to be surrounded, but just accepted as dead and taken off at the end of the game as prisoners.

But let me show you how White can kill if forced to do so. This happens when the surrounding stones are themselves being surrounded and a race to capture starts. When White plays first, he puts Black in atari :

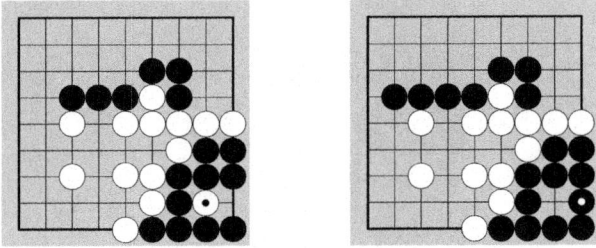

Now there is a single point. Black has one liberty left. White can play there to kill because it takes all Black liberties away. So this is when a move is not deemed to be suicide as it completes the surrounding of a group of stones:

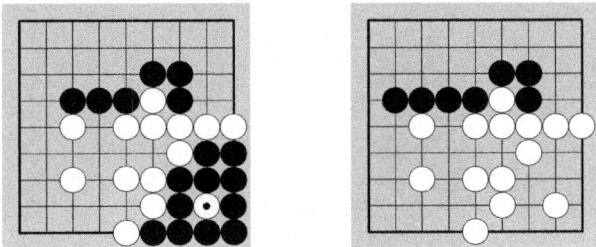

Black has 1 prisoner, and White now has 11 prisoners. Now if we play to completion, the result is very different :

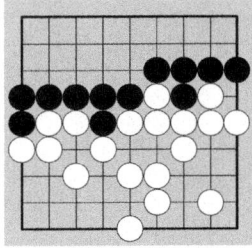

Black has 23 stones on the upper size as before, plus 1 prisoner to have a total of 24 points. White has 26 points on the lower side, plus 11 prisoners to have a total of 37 points. So White wins by 13 points plus komi.

This should give you a tiny taster of the game of Go. Its profound richness has entranced millions for centuries. On the full sized 19 by 19 line board, strategy, tactics and creativity are required in equal measure!

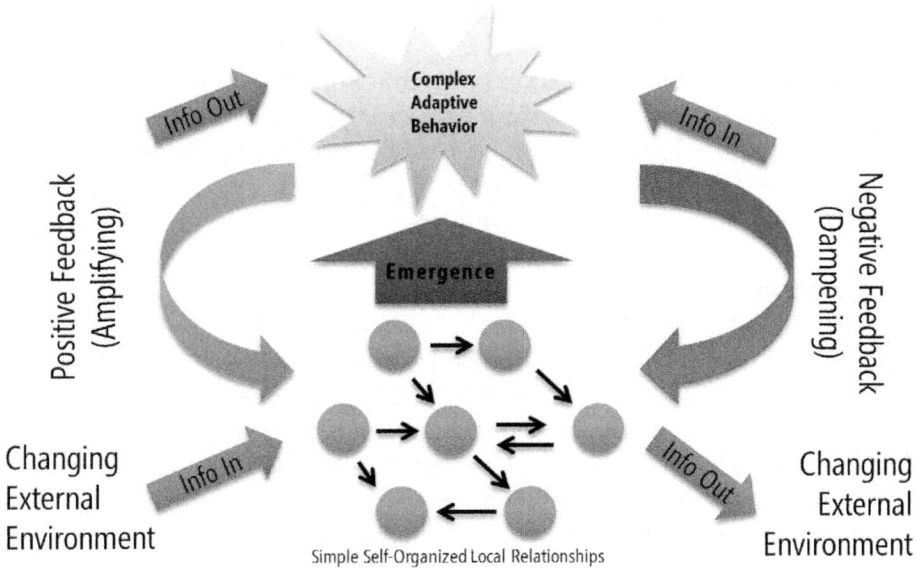

Positive Feedback (Amplifying)

Negative Feedback (Dampening)

Info Out

Info In

Complex Adaptive Behavior

Emergence

Info In

Info Out

Changing External Environment

Changing External Environment

Simple Self-Organized Local Relationships

Complex systems

Complex systems are everywhere
Your body is one
Society is another
Yet they are badly understood by most of us

They are surprisingly relevant, often countero-intuitive and one of my favourite subjects. I hope to show you why.

Kate Raworth makes this tricky subject appear simple, using succinct anecdotes more often than many writers feel appropriate :

> At the heart of systems thinking lie three deceptively simple concepts: stocks and flows, feedback loops and delay. They sound straightforward enough but the mind-boggling business begins when they start to interact. Out of their interplay emerge many of the surprising, extraordinary and unpredictable events in the world.

If you have ever been mesmerised by the sight of thousands of starlings flocking at sunset – in a spectacle poetically known as a murmuration – then you'll know just how extraordinary such 'emergent properties' can be. Each bird twists and turns in flight, using phenomenal agility to stay a mere wingspan apart from its neighbours, while tilting as they tilt. But as tens of thousands of birds gather together, all following these same simple rules, the flock as a whole becomes an astonishing swooping, pulsing mass flowing across the night sky.

So what is a system? Simply a set of things that are interconnected in ways that produce distinct patterns of behaviour – be they cells in an organism, protestors in a crowd, birds in a flock, members of a family, or banks in a financial network. And it is the relationships between the individual parts – shaped by their stocks and flows, feedbacks and delays – that give rise to their emergent behaviour.

Stocks and flows

These are the basic elements of any system: things that can get built up or run down – just like water in a bath, fish in the sea, people on the planet, trust in a community, or money on the bank. A stock's levels change over time due to the balance between its inflows and outflows. A bathtub fills or empties depending on how fast water pours in from the tap versus how fast it drains out of the plughole. A flock of chickens grows or shrinks depending on the rate of chicks born versus chickens dying. A piggy bank fills up if more coins are added than are taken away.

Feedback loops

If stocks and flows are a system's core elements, then feedback loops are their interconnections, and in every system there are two kinds: *reinforcing* (or 'positive') feedback loops and *balancing* ('negative') ones. With reinforcing feedback loops, the more you have, the more you get. They amplify what is happening, creating vicious or virtuous circles that will, if unchecked, lead either to explosive growth or to collapse. Chickens lay eggs, which hatch into chickens, and so the poultry population grows and grows. Likewise, in the vengeful tit-for-tat of playground fights, a single rough shove can soon escalate into a full-blown bust-up. Interest earned on savings adds to those savings, increasing those savings, increasing future interest payments, and so wealth accumulates. But reinforcing feedback can lead to collapse too: the less you have, the less you get. If people lose confidence in their bank and withdraw their savings, for example, it will start to run out of cash, deepening the loss of confidence and leading to a run on the bank.

If *reinforcing* feedbacks are what make a system move, then *balancing* feedbacks are what stop it from exploding or imploding. They counter and offset what is happening, and so tend to regulate systems. Our bodies use balancing feedbacks to maintain a healthy temperature: get too hot and your skin will start sweating in order to cool you down; get too cold and your body will start shivering in an attempt to warm itself up. A household's thermostat works in a similar way to stabilise room temperature. In effect, balancing feedbacks bring stability to a system.

Delays

Delays between inflows and outflow, such as the rate at which you spend your income and receive new pay cheques – are common in systems and can have big effects. Sometimes they bring useful stability to a system, where stocks build up to act as buffers or shock absorbers : think energy stored in a battery, food in the cupboard, or savings in the bank. But stock-flow delays can produce system stubbornness too : no matter how much effort gets put in, it takes time, say, to reforest a hillside, build trust in a community, or improve a school's exam grades. And delay can generate big oscillations when systems are slow to respond – as anyone knows who has been scalded then frozen again while trying to master the taps on an unfamiliar shower.

It is out of these interactions of stock, flows, feedbacks and delays that complex adaptive systems arise: complex due to their unpredictable emergent behaviour, and adaptive because they keep evolving over time. Beyond these matters, it soon becomes clear just how powerful systems thinking can be for understanding our ever-evolving world, from the rise of corporate empires to the collapse of ecosystems. Many events that first appear to be sudden and external – what mainstream economists often describe as 'exogenous shocks' – are far better understood as arising from endogenous change. In the words of the political economist Orit Gal, 'complexity theory teaches us that major events are the manifestation of maturing and converging underlying trends: they reflect change that has already occurred with the system'.

From this perspective, the 1989 fall of the Berlin Wall, the 2008 collapse of Lehman Brothers and the imminent collapse of the Greenland Ice sheet have much in common. All three are reported in the news as sudden events but are actually visible tipping points that result from slowly accumulated pressure in the system – be it the gradual growth of political protest in Eastern Europe, the build-up of sub-prime mortgages in a bank's asset portfolio, or the accumulation of greenhouse gases in the atmosphere. As Donella Meadows, one of the early champions of systems thinking, put it :

> *Let's face it, the universe is messy. It is nonlinear, turbulent and chaotic. It is dynamic. It spends its time in transient behaviour on its way to somewhere else, not in mathematically neat equilibria. It self-organises and evolves. It creates diversity, not uniformity. That's what makes the world interesting, that's what makes it beautiful, and that's what makes it work.*

An evolutionary tale
An abridged version of a short Utopian novel

I had been blessed with occasional lucid dreams over the years. To be conscious while asleep. Quite the paradox! This consciousness was confined to the cinema in my head, but unlike real cinemas, here I could choose how the script panned out. Sometimes I would conjure up a lady to hug. Immensely realistic, it would mostly overexcite me, rapidly waking me up. Other times, I would check how realistic the 3D imagery was. One such time I was on a bus and the scenery shooting past was even rendered plausibly in the water drops on the window pane. It always baffled me that my brain could generate such realism absent sensory inputs. No amount of searching online yielded an explanation.

But the lucidity of the dream I found myself in was tangibly different. This felt more realistic. Maybe half-way between dreaming and real life. Was this an hallucination? Maybe this was a window into another world or even another time. I now noticed that the music in the room had faded away. It was replaced by the sound of a voice. A most pleasant female voice.

"Hello. Are you OK? You look a bit lost" said a lady who had appeared in front of me. Except that she did not say those exact words. This was the gist of what she actually said. She spoke in a kind of English that sounded archaic. For ease of reading, I will translate for you, as I did above.

Dreams can be a bit strange like that, I thought, offering a flawed mimicry of reality. But on reflection, however, I decided that there seemed meaning in the way the words sounded differently. Not some random gameplay by my mind.

Dreams can become hyper real – when we enter a state of *lucidity* where we actually become conscious whilst dreaming.

It can feel exquisite to be so profoundly aware of proceedings in these internal, fabricated worlds. Not only that, but we soon learn that we are able to steer them! Vivid contrivances of our choice can instantly be manifested. But I initially wanted to see how this dream or hallucination panned out without any overt force of my own applied. I decided that I would play along with it as far as I could because it felt so tangibly more realistic than even lucid dreams, and I did not want to risk it fading away. Which of course now meant that a reply was overdue to the question being asked of me.

"Hello. I am OK and very much lost." I replied using the only variant of English that I knew.

"How odd you sound. Where did you learn to speak in this way?" she asked.

"I was going to ask you the same question. I can mostly understand you but you speak as if you have added and changed words at random. As if a foreigner was trying to speak English."

"And to my ears, you speak as the ancients used to." she replied.

This was not the most welcome of dialogues with a stranger in a potentially strange land. I looked around and all that unfolded before me was super clear and vivid. Lucid dreams are almost as real as real life if this was one.

It always baffled me that I could stand in the middle of countryside in a lucid dream that was unfamiliar, yet inspection of any part even small, like the bark of a tree would be rendered in great detail. How on earth could my mind hold this level of detail? I scoured the internet a number of times to see if anyone could shed a light on this matter. But to no avail.

In a number of lucid dreams, I made a point of moving my head left and right to see how the scene responded in three dimensions. The answer was invariably 'flawlessly plausible'. My brain could not hold videos of each scene taken from the different angles I now adopted. It has always felt like a lucid dream was a portal to somewhere beyond the confines of my mind.

We were in the middle of a street in this 'dream'. Except that there was no road. Nor any cars. The grass stretched between lines of neatly maintained gardens that fronted houses that looked more Norwegian than British. Bold blue and yellow timber framed creations. I suspected, at first, that this must be a wealthy neighbourhood as all the houses were detached. Except that there was no real grandeur, and some of these properties were single storey. Bungalows, I guessed. Some were truly tiny. Many houses had what must be solar panels, but they looked rather different because they did not comprise separate panels, but one single unit. A few houses had grass growing on flat roofs, and one of the tiny houses was actually best described as a mud hut. Maybe it was the novelty of difference, but the smaller the house, the greater the appeal it had to me.

I described lines of houses. This was not strictly correct as the road actually curved like a ribbon. What need, I concluded, for straight lines when there are no cars? It reminded me of the price we pay in 'my time' for land smothered in hardened tarmac and concrete that bore moving and many very static cars. Absent these vehicles, the air of course felt fresher also.

There were trees in what would have been the middle of a road. The biggest of these had a wide girth around which was constructed, with a labour of love, the most exquisite oak wood circular bench where the backs formed a wave like the ocean, circling the tree. Another tree further along was clearly bearing fruit, but they looked like a cross between apples and bananas! Beneath the tree was a layer of soft, spongy material, on top of which sat a couple of 'apples'. Not only did this also seem to serve the public rather than sit privately behind a wall in someone's garden, but it was clearly intentionally *planned* to serve the public, the sponge minimising bruising when the fruits dropped.

My word, this was a most fascinating and intriguing place to behold. But to be a part of it was all the more special of course.

A little further down the road there were some children playing. Except, of course, it was not a road. It was like a narrow, winding, meandering park sprinkled with those tress and also a few benches. Next to one bench was a fresh water dispenser. I struggled to recall when I last saw such a creature-comfort available in a public area. Most such niceties were not welcomed by coffee shops, so tended to get squeezed away by the imperative for private profit acquisition.

The lady I had been talking with was in her early 30's I presumed, wearing a kind of tracksuit in a pale lavender colour. She was pretty, with a tussled mop of slightly untidy brown hair. And a calm demeanour. The conversation might have been awkward, but less so because of the manner in which she delivered her words. She was very much Scandinavian in demeanour, but was clearly English by upbringing.

"Can you tell me where I am?" I asked, my curiosity piqued by what I saw.

"You really must be lost then. This is Odiham, near Old Basingstoke."

I knew of this village, but my scant memory did not accord in any way with what lay before my eyes. That assumed, however, that what I was observing was in fact sourced by my vision. Maybe it was a rich contrivance. Certainly a vivid and convincingly real one.

"This may be a stupid question, but what year is it?" I asked.

"Not only are you lost in space but you seem equally lost in time. It is Day 10.4 in the year 578." she replied.

Well that answered one question for sure. This was one crazy dream or hallucination. Too far-fetched for me to have been transported somewhere, or to have a connection with another place. Maybe I was thinking too simplistically. But I was also starting to feel scared. The novelty was wearing off, and the sheer realism was making me feel as if I had become permanently displaced spatially and temporally. A fish out of water, and out of time, even if in pleasant surroundings.

"You look a bit pale right now. Your mouth dropped when I told you the date. Maybe you are from the time before the date and day system was unlinked from the purported birth of Christ? There is a hexagon just up the way here where we can sit and talk about that with a hot drink." she kindly offered, her arm linking into mine.

I did not resist, not least because such genuine but gentle intimacy always had a profound effect on me. This was the other side of the social anxiety coin – when social harmony prevailed, I sensed that I felt it more warmly and intensely than those who managed to avoid the poison of chronic anxiety. My experience of life is in effect amplified, for both good and bad.

She explained to my 21st century novice mind that a hexagon was a hub where eight grass ways converged. I could see that in the centre was something fortunately familiar, giving a comforting feeling of the known in this alien land. It was a bandstand, itself also hexagonal in structure, sat atop a small mound of grass with seats all around in three concentric hexagonals. Further back were eight rows of shops, restaurants and cafes.

I checked in my pockets and I had no money, not that I expected to be thus equipped. So I hoped that she would pay. But I realised we had not even exchanged names, or, dare I inquire, jobs.

"My name is James, what is yours, and what is your job or occupation?"

"Hello James. It has been interesting to meet you. My name is Lofarian. We can talk about work when we get seated."

It occurred to me as we walked that in dreams I never see my feet. So I looked down and there they were. They were clad in strange looking but exquisitely comfortable shoes. They made the grass feel soft with each step that I took. I was also wearing some unusual pale blue one-piece leisure-wear. I felt sure that my imagination would not have conjured up this appearance. But my introspecting was abruptly interrupted by the sound of a child in distress.

Lofarian yanked my arm and we ran towards the distraught girl, now crying as she sat on the grass, nursing a sore arm. She had been running near a bench while being chased by a boy, and her forearm had caught the top corner of the bench back. There was no bleeding but it was raw red.

"Are you OK?" Lofarian asked as we approached. "Just rest a moment and then I can take you home. Do you live nearby?"

The girl, now calmer, pointed to her house which was just a little way down the way. Two storey, painted in a tempered beige colour. (Why, I wondered, centuries ahead the houses looked so basic and even familiar?) The girl bade farewell to her friends who wished her a speedy recovery.

It was all very polite and mannered. Especially so for such young children, the girl most likely no older than six. It reminded me of the golden era of Shepparton and Ealing studios films in the 50's. Children in these black and white productions were even polite and respectful towards the ever visible policeman on the beat. There was often a gentleness of human relationships that seems to have been replaced by a social distancing from others in modern life (the life that felt suspended for me now), where it was deemed quite acceptable to walk the streets with head bowed in subservience to a mobile phone, and hearing tuned into music from headphones. You cannot even say hello to these people.

We walked to this wonderful looking house, Lofarian's left hand holding my arm, and her right hand holding the left hand of the child, whose name was Iris.

A subtle surprise was next on the agenda. The front door to her house was pushed open with no key required for there was no lock. Just a simple pull-down handle. Maybe it was the weekend, but as we entered we could see both parents were at home. They greeted us warmly, and crouched down to Iris to speak with her and tend to her injury. As they did so, I took the opportunity to scan the room we were in. Presumably what I would call a lounge. There was no sign of a television, but one wall looked like it could possibly be a super large screen. The seating certainly faced it, and it was devoid of hanging pictures. The furniture itself looked elegantly functional, making me feel disappointed in a way that centuries ahead things were not vastly different. There was certainly less clutter

95

and, I realised, not a single mobile phone or electronic gadget in sight so far.

There was a quiet calm in this room, even though the front door was still open. This was simply because there was no dull throbbing sound of traffic outside. Yet it was not completely silent, for there was the distant sound of children playing and the tweeting music of birdsong from the trees. This did not stop the sense of quiet, but merely imbued it with a gentleness largely alien to my era.

Somehow, though, this ambience sounded familiar. On due reflection, I recalled precisely this clear, unmasked sound of birdsong during the first few days of lockdown in 2020 in response to the Corona Virus pandemic. As then, the serenity was subtly but tangibly appealing. It was starting to make the intensity of life I was used to seem already to begin to feel alien. Much like what happens on the first day on a holiday, with the sun beating down on a reclined body, adaptation to calm bliss a remarkably swift matter.

Lofarian bade me a farewell while Iris received first aid from her father.

"Thanks for helping bring Iris home. It was good of you. Can I offer you a coffee?" he asked.

Of course I was most happy to accept, and to sit with these 'aliens'. I had become embroiled with my situation now, even though a part of me realised it was probably a fantasy. Much as I do when engrossed in a good film. But when it was this plausible and real, I could not help but get drawn into the part I was now 'playing'. I was unavoidably an actor in this movie.

"I am Eric, this is Dora and my rescued daughter goes by the name of Iris. What is your name? I ask as your face does not seem familiar and I know pretty much everyone in the hamlet." he continued as we sat down to enjoy coffees and, unusually, a bowl of grapes.

Now there was a term I had not expected from a future scenario. A hamlet is supposed to be a small village, but this seemed rather more substantial. I gave him my name and declared that I was 'visiting' the area, a curiously honest reply from my perspective.

I learnt that he was a landscape gardener, cabinet maker, teacher and drummer. And that Dora was a chef, mechanical design engineer and spiritual leader. I presumed that one of these roles was their principle job, but this presumption was swiftly quashed. Despite being in their 30's, neither of them had a job. They did not need to earn a living from all that they did as the state supplied all their needs for free – she referred to it as the *Collective*. This was hard to grasp. It made the 21st century concept of *Universal Basic Income* seem like a half-baked idea.

"I just cannot understand this. How can the state supply all your needs? " I asked.

He did not reply directly but first sought to get a frame of reference for me. It was most clear to him that I was out of touch, to say the very least, and that he needed to know what my knowledge base was. And precisely where indeed I was from. And *when* I was from.

I refused to say that I was an ancient, and this allowed him to at least temper the cognitive dissonance created by realising that someone from centuries ago was sat in front of him. But he was certainly very wary of me at the same time as being a little excited.

"Will you be able to meet with my colleague Brian next week? He works in ancient history studies at the research centre in Cobbleton a few miles from here?" he asked.

"You are welcome to stay for a meal today – my wife will shortly start to make her 4th day special. A mixed bean curry with ginger infused rice." he followed.

I agreed to both, realising that the authenticity of the scene unravelling before my senses also included my own bodily needs. I realised that I was ravenous! As I waited to eat, Eric and I just chatted. There was no TV or phone to distract us. Iris sat and watched us with clear interest. This felt a little like a throw-back to the 1950's and I wondered if we would start singing around a piano sometime soon.

As we were eating a most delicious but fairly simple meal, notably absent animal products, I was thinking ahead. If I am as stuck here as I seem now to be, where on earth would I sleep? What would I do for money and food and a job. OK, a job did not seem to be needed. But money surely. Unless the Collective would pay me a living wage even as an alien visitor?

My attention kept returning to Iris. Occasionally, she would join in the conversation, but her mind clearly did not wander away when merely listening. There was a sense of an adult level of attention. After she had finished her main meal, her mother started whispering in her ear. Normally, we avert our eyes when this happens, but she did not. She was still moving her attention between myself and Eric as our dialogue bounced back and forth. Just as her mother moved away, Iris declared :

"I think you are being a bit modest there dad. You always helped out. Not just on that one occasion."

It seemed like she was rudely ignoring her mother, except for what she said next
:

"Mum has asked me to help prepare desert. I think you will be in for a surprise!".

No child I knew could do this. Not just listen to and heed what her mother says, but do so whilst seemingly actively listening to our conversation. On the surface, this seemed a small matter. But its sheer rarity in my experience made it stand out like a sore thumb. Was Iris a gifted child, he wondered. Sure, she was smart, but beyond smart, maybe?

Left alone with Eric, my concerns about the night looming ahead were then to be delightfully assuaged.

"I am guessing that you are a long way from home and not sure of a room for the night. Excuse me if this is a bad misjudgement." he said.

"If I am right, I offer you a room for the night."

"You are right, and no offence was therefore taken. This is most generous. I barely know you and I am welcomed into your house with more dignity and generosity than some of my friends would offer me. But this is your house and I am still a stranger. I feel that you are being too generous." I replied.

"Not at all!" he exclaimed.

"This is my house and it is not my house. It is my chosen house, but owned by the state. I do not pay rent. It is part of the collective. No one owns their homes."

"But what about rich people who want a larger, more resplendent property maybe with a swimming pool and tennis court?" I asked.

"There are no rich people. But we are treading into the territory I want you to discuss with Brian. My suspicion is that you are somehow an ancient out of his time, even if you do not confirm that, and also that such a reality simply makes no sense. It is just my instinct reacting to the way you are responding to your surroundings that makes me think this way." he replied.

So it was that I was able to go to sleep in a house in the future while presumably hallucinating. I guessed for sure that my awakening would be back in my own time.

But truth is that I did wake up in my new home.

This put a more serious connotation on my experience. The lucidity was both consistently coherent and sustained. This was no dream scenario fluttering by. It was an entrenched state now. At least it seemed to be, feeling scarily like real life.

But it was hard to be truly frightened as I was guest of the most delightful and welcoming of families. What was there to be frightened of? A great deal of course. I was out of time and place, losing something we hold most precious in our lives – some agency over my destiny. But most likely this was an hallucination, even if of the highest order, so I could just presume that and let the fear calm down and replace it with a sense of adventure. We do this on holiday in a strange land, so why not now? Live and enjoy each moment as a precious escape from so much monotony of normal daily life.

Breakfast was weird. Because there was no breakfast. Dora explained that the human body awakens to a state of activity and the last thing it needs is to blunt that with food. So most people missed breakfast these days. Instead, I joined them in a trip to what was best described as an allotment. A communal fruit and vegetable plot, at the end of the 'road' in the opposite direction to the Hexagon. But the sheer size of it and the presence of seating areas and a cafe gave it an entirely different flavour. Dora had supplied me with some thick gardening clothes and tough but thin gloves. Even Iris was happy to join in.

And boy was it fun! And tiring. My back ached so badly after the hour or so we spent mostly doubled over digging, weeding and occasionally lifting some tubers. The plot, if I could still call this vast area that, was not owned by the community. No one owned a slice of land. It was all owned by the collective, for all to toil and share. But, I wondered, would there be lazy, greedy people taking more than their fair share? Scanning around it was hard to see this happening. Everyone seemed to be content working, even if some took frequent breaks.

I decided to wander around after half an hour of toil, having checked with my hosts to verify this was acceptable. And this allows me to explain how poor my use of the word 'allotment' really had been. The land being cultivated stretched for about a mile in each direction. Just as with the hexagon at the centre of the 'roads' there was an elevated area at the centre of this land with 8 pathways leading from it, at 45 degree intervals. The two main arteries had railway tracks on them, with pedal driven vehicles traversing them. At the customary sedentary pace. This presumably allowed the less mobile to travel the large distances involved in transporting themselves and their produce. The other paths were for walking.

The raised centre circular area commanded a fabulous view over the land. There were deckchairs and even some hammocks. This was like a holiday resort more than public land. It made me wonder why we had such spartan seating arrangements in public areas in my time.

I walked along one of these main paths (there were also smaller paths of course between banks of crops). I reached one of the enclosed areas. It appeared to be designed and constructed in pretty much the same manner as our poly-tunnels. Reassuring proof that elegant design can indeed stand the test of time. I opened the door and entered, bathed as I did by a wave of moist warm air. This was like Kew Gardens! The humidity was infused with earthy, peppery smells. This felt kind of addictive. The place you would yearn for when toiling away at work. Again, though, I had to remind myself that this was in fact what they did for work. Their pleasure in cultivating foods was part of the community collective. They were growing tomatoes and even some corn in this 'greenhouse'.

Another enclosure I encountered was as tall as this one was long. Venturing inside I found myself face to face with a fifty foot high Avocado plant, replete with avocados. How truly wonderful.

I returned to my hosts with some haste as I had spent rather a while in my explorations. They were not angry. It felt like they would struggle to be angry with anything.

When we were finished, we meandered over to the cafe zone. The very notion of meandering seemed to encapsulate this time I found myself in. There was not rush. Everyone seemed to have time on their hands. Which of course made sense if no one had a formal job. On top of that, the snacks and coffee were free. How good is that? So I allowed for the compromise that cakes and cookies were not to be seen. The 'snacks' were little bowls of mixed fruit and vegetables. And the coffee was not coffee. Nor was it made with milk. It had barley and nutmeg tones. But was OK, and besides, who was I to be fussy? Before we left, Eric gave a bundle of carrots and potatoes to the young lady serving at the cafe. This was no market exchange but a non-reciprocal thing – a number of people dropped off fruit and veg as they sat there without stopping to indulge.

To my sensibilities, this was no advanced society but one that had regressed to more primitive ways. I chewed on the situation as we walked – again at a snail's pace – back to the house. Maybe advanced did not mean technically so, but practically so. I asked Eric how a world without work succeeded when it had been pounded into my head that mass employment and the economy were vital to a good standard of living. Suffice to say was that he had to 'enlighten' me about the nature of propaganda that suited those 'in charge' at the expense of the public at large. A continuance of the old feudal master-slave regime but in a (thin) disguise.

When we got back, Eric said that he had heard back from Brian who he assured me would give better answers to such questions. He must have contacted him last night before I went to bed. Did they still use mobile phones I wondered. Or computers. They had to. Anyway, it appeared that Brian was so intrigued by the potential goldmine of information that I might offer as a living relic from the past that he wanted to see me today. This very morning in fact.

I agreed and we set off for the levitation station. That was something I really had to see and experience! With all the walking and 'gardening' I was quite tired and achy, but I felt wonderfully alive. The slow pace in this era seemed to have a benign side-effect of making me more in tune with and aware of my surroundings. My mind less cluttered, the air clean and pure, I was able to truly see and smell the trees and bushes that we passed. Honeysuckle smelled exquisite, as if I had never really smelt it properly before. The instinct now acquired to pause and smell a rose was equally well rewarded. I also noticed each step that I was taking. The cadence of my walking somehow felt 'correct' and rhythmic.

The station was, alas, a low-key affair. There was a queue of train 'pods' along a siding. The idea was to board the most advanced, as if at a taxi rank. It seated six people, with room for a few more standing. There was only four of us, but this was apparently fine, the minimum for the vehicle to start when the doors were closed was three. Needless to say there was no fee collection for our journey.

It paused a while to allow for another pod to whoosh past on the main line going East via Cobbleton. Our pod wobbled slightly to and fro before slowly starting up, silently. It swung from the siding onto the main track and ramped up to full speed.

The countryside was beautiful, flowing past at a fair but not excessive speed. The occasional village was to be seen but there was a conspicuous absence of tarmac, or any other ghastly mankind smear on the landscape. Levitated above the guide rail, only the wind rushing past was generating any sound.

Cobbleton proved slightly anti-climatic, much like a clone of the hamlet I had just left, but with the first building of any substantial size was evident in the distance. It was indeed the research centre where Brian worked. The focal point of this small town it transpired. As we walked, I asked Eric :

"You said that no one worked, but there must be people making and maintaining systems, like the train we took. And providing medical care and building houses. And so on!"

101

"Of course. My apologies for confusing the matter. Brian will explain more fully, but I really should have said that there are no longer any paid employees. The work is done but not via 40 hour working weeks. Things are way more flexible now as you will discover. Brian will explain how and why things got to this state." he replied.

I was being primed nicely for what would seem to be as exciting a rendezvous for me as for Brian. He was standing outside the research centre to greet us. Either he was a very patient man, or he was savvy about the timing of our journey. Eric introduced me, and said he would return in a couple of hours to meet up again.

Brian's smile was as relaxed as his demeanour. If such nature was a signature of the era, then I was that much keener to hear more. I presumed that Brian knew as much about current times as historic ones. When we got seated with cups of green tea and sunflower seeds to crack open and nibble on, I immediately asked Brian why his research was not deemed to be a job or work. But he first wanted to make me feel welcome, and I felt a little guilty for bypassing etiquette :

"Nice to meet you James. You have no idea how excited I am to meet you but also how scared I am that my excitement may be ill-founded. It is, of course, far more likely that you are of the current era than someone implausibly transported from ancient times fully *compos mentis*. But Eric tells me that he senses a consistency in your awe about how things are in our times." Brian said.

"And great to meet you Brian. Thanks for taking your time. Sorry for the abruptness of my question. I suspect we both have many. And yes, I am not of this time, but my suspicion matches yours in a sense. I am deeply unsure why I am here and that this is a reality that could be happening. It feels like I am hallucinating. Except, that is, for the stark sense of sustained realism." I replied.

"Why do you think you are hallucinating? By the way, I would guess from your nature that you are an open minded guy, but I want to check that you are open to questions. I have many ..."

"Sure, sure. Fire away. The very simple answer is that I had taken a hallucinogenic drug. A psychedelic that can trigger all kinds of changes in the mind, including vivid imagery. But unless that altered state took me to some kind of gateway to a parallel or alternate universe, I cannot explain nor understand my experience in this here and now." I replied.

"Before we go on, can I get that original question off my chest in case I forget it?" I asked.

"You are kind – I really appreciate your openness. I will proceed on the assumption that you are from an ancient time, even though why or how are unknowns." he replied.

"Both work and education were what I describe as *monolithic* systems in the 20th and 21st centuries that you know. One dimensional strait-jackets that failed to recognise, expand and nourish the multi-dimensional nature within us and the vast diversities across us. A single job that tied us to one or a small spectrum of our interests and capabilities for too many hours each day and week. Education systems that chained us in quietude in front of an authority figure that tried to pour facts into our bored and unwilling minds, killing or bypassing our passions and compromising natural development."

Brian was on full throttle now. But these words resonated with me.

"Essentially, education and work had been commandeered by those who wanted to control and exploit the public. School was a conditioning system, plying us to accept near-slave treatment in the work place." he continued.

But I interrupted :

"Now hold on a minute. This seems a bit extreme. And it certainly does not hold true for the Nordic countries, for example, where children have structured play until formal education starts at age seven. And that this education is more egalitarian than constraining. And many businesses treated their workers with exemplary fairness and respect."

"Yes, yes, yes, and sorry. You are of course correct. I was falling into a generalisation trap. We now have no employers or jobs. But we do work. Except that we do not see the concept in the same way. Post climate-change-recovery, we re-envisaged many things. We saw that the notion of legitimising activities as meaningful work *only* when they paid was an insanely unbalanced way to cultivate a civilised society. Surely, caring for an ailing or inform family member was also work? A hobby repairing things for neighbours for free was also work. So we re-conceived as in an activity that achieved something of value for ourselves or others. And we dropped the name in the process" he continued.

"Now, it has become 'just' an activity. Like picking up litter. Like cutting your grass. Like helping carry the shopping for an elderly man. Like carrying out surgery to fix a broken bone. Like cultivating food."

He was in full swing now, and I felt I dared not interrupt him.

"Suddenly, we were free to do a diversity of things each day, no longer shackled to a desk or the same routines for 40 hours." he finished, allowing me to reply.

"You mean to say that no-one is being paid anymore?" I asked.

"Not directly, no. They receive what they need from the collective. A kind of form of Communism in your era terms."

"But Communism has failed wherever it was deployed. What makes it, or a variant of it work now?" I asked.

"A prudent question. The answer is complex and multifaceted. Let me show you around the research centre first and then please give me time to mull over our conversation." he replied.

My eyes lit up when he showed me the library! This was heaven – not just books, but books out of my world! I asked for his tour to stop immediately so that I could indulge myself. And, strangely, he agreed to my sudden request. What a tolerant fellow.

Later, Eric rejoined us and we went to the restaurant in the research centre. A fairly basic but seemingly nutritious self service vegan offering from what I could tell. I guessed that animal welfare was also challenged in a similar vein to how education and work were. The habit of breeding other sentient creatures just so that we could butcher and eat them! I say this as a meat, fish and poultry eater. But an increasingly reluctant one now.

There was no one to take payment for our food. Yet no one was exploiting this by over-eating. The near-sedentary speed of life seemed matched by this absence of intense over-indulging.

We went outside afterwards to sit in some lounge chairs in a picturesque garden, swamped in colour. But there was enough greenery to help calm my excited mind. I found it hard to believe anyone else might have an hallucination remotely as fascinating as this one. All the more reason to believe that I was somewhere that really did have its own existence.

Brian explained to Eric where we had reached in our chat, and resumed his narrative. He had a lot to say, but I really did wonder why a researcher of ancient times would be asking questions rather than answering them.

"I want to go right back to a time in the past that was also a history even for you. The time when man was principally a hunter-gatherer – when he roamed for a few hours each day to hunt down game. The sheer practicalities of this process meant that they would not want to reverse that route to return home. So they frequently relocated and carried very few possessions. Food was shared more by need than by the prowess of the hunters. Inequality was almost non-existent." Brian started out.

"Man eventually discovered the value of agriculture and farming, and hunting went into decline. Fixed dwellings were now viable and assets – material possessions – they could contain likewise became viable. And plentiful. A sense of ownership crept in. Some claimed land as their own and became powerful, enabling more land acquisition by force. The very notion of ownership on the back of sewing seeds also sewed the seed of increasing inequality. Markets allowed different tribes to effectively exchange goods. Some exchanges were not possible because of the timing of the creation or growing of goods, so money became a means of deferring exchanges."

"I am giving a fast history here, but we will be here all day otherwise. Suffice to say, you are aware of the perversion of the role of money as a means of evening out the timings on the exchange of goods. It was, almost inevitably, something that sadly became leveraged. Exploited. It was too powerful and became an asset to covet as much as land and property. Feudal times saw the rise of a master-slave inequality on the back of asset and power acquisition. Wealth spawned more wealth in a positive, exponential manner, much as the poverty of the slaves to the wealthy compounded negatively. The lure of wealth and power was a powerful force. Those that acquired both struggled immensely to let go – to share with those less fortunate."

This was also pretty familiar material. I had read deeply about these things. Brian continued :

"The middle ages saw an uprising of the masses against the oppression of feudalism. Years of fighting eventually restored a pre-feudal egalitarian state, where the powerful were effectively dethroned. But that did not last terribly long. 'Enclosure' acts were passed that saw public land return into the private hands of a few powerful figures and once again, the many became shackled as workers for the few, needing employment because of property loss. The Capitalism that evolved from this grew, with Corporatism, to dominate the planet. Instead of relative equality and egalitarianism, and a harmony with the land, businesses exploited the planet as a free source of materials and dump of waste products in much the same way they treated the workers. This eventually lead to excess carbon dioxide emissions that destabilised the climate. Your era sits in the very heat of the effects of that disastrous misuse and abuse of the planet for private profit. There is a book on how climate change was combatted in the library. And another on what grew from the massive global change in zeitgeist, not least the dethroning of the self-serving powerful. I'll dig them out to lend to you before you go." he continued.

"That was some condensation of history, but you have my due respect. Rather a lot to take in even so. But thanks. I did indeed see a book entitled 'The arresting of climate change'. Was that the one?" I asked.

"Yup. The other one is the rather badly entitled 'A new world order'." Brian replied.

"You will be better positioned to continue this chat after reading those books. What say you?" he asked.

Of course I snapped at the idea. Before leaving with these precious books, Brian interrogated me about my life and era. I would guess we spoke for the better part of two hours. He absorbed what I said with an eagerness more befitting a child in a sweetshop. But I understood that, of course.

I was again inordinately grateful that I could stay another night with Eric's family, and that this offer was so relaxed and effortlessly offered. I was growing attached to this family and this time and place.

But before we parted, he added a few more words about the past – my past – that informed decision making post-apocalypse, to set the scene for that 2nd book :

"For most of the 300,000 years humans have been roaming around looking pretty much like we do, they lived with an animism ontology. They felt connected with and at one with the other living creatures."

This reminded me of the sense of correctness I felt in my first psychedelic trip where I felt at one with the Universe. Something very fundamental to feel. At the root of human existence yet lost to most of us these days. Or, rather, my days. He continued :

"Feudalism not only needed to make slaves of the many, but to get them to believe that this was a natural order of life. The church also needed to compromise the sense of the collective that the animism ontology created. To survive, they needed people to see the path to God as the only connection they needed.

Yet before feudalism, humans lived and worked only to serve their needs and desires and not to furnish overlords with vast wealth. They holidayed a lot and celebrated life with many festivals. There were no extremes of wealth – equality was in a healthy state.

When resources are constrained by nature, or as with feudalism and capitalism by man himself, living beings have to fight for survival shares. When primates split between chimpanzees and bonobos, separated onto different land masses, one scarce of resources the other replete, these creatures evolved very differently. The bonobos became a highly sociable, relaxed species, whereas in the endless fight for resources, the chimps could and would attack each other at will.

What grew out of the climate crisis was an International organisation called C.O.P.E. – the Custodians Of Planet Earth. In light of lessons learned in the past as I have just detailed, they established a few fundamental principles across the planet to avoid any future such catastrophes. The root principle was that no one owned anything. No land, no buildings, no nothing. It was all part of the collective. And that means no money. Or wealth. Or power. And no psychopaths around anyway to be attracted to these things.

After sharing another vegan meal with my host, I spent pretty much the whole of the remainder of the evening devouring the first of these books. They alone were among the most exciting things I had encountered so far in my whole life. Glimpses, potentially, into my own future. But would I be able to remember what I read here when I finally 'woke up' back there in my real life?

Part of my rapturous joy with these books was the sheer sensuous touch of their velvety covers. But why paperback books in this advanced era? How about deforestation? Of course, I noticed on the back of the book that the paper was made from hemp – a very fast growing wood substitute plant. The colour rendition on both of the covers and inside these books was magnificent. Much like a smart phone screen from my era. Before I even started reading I was in heaven.

I will give highlights from the books, attempting to summarise what was an epochal, seismic period of transition, when a phoenix arose from planet-wide flames.

The climate change book was to be a 'history' book of the current era that would be a history, present and future book for me. It started by discussing the UNFCC, the United Nations Framework Convention on Climate Change, established in 1992. It was the first international recognition and action on the effects of carbon dioxide emissions damaging the climate that had been know for at least three decades by then. It set in process a series of climate change conferences that were supposed to mete out the required changes to all countries to implement. Back in 2021, the 26th 'Conference of the parties' was about to start.

But nearly three decades had elapsed with precious few meaningful recommendations agreed and actually undertaken. So that emissions were still rising. There were simply too many business and countries with heavy ties to fossil fuels and therefore to the continuation of the status quo. 'Someone else, more guilty', like China, needs to start changing its habits before I should need to change mine, the sentiment went. China's conversion to a form of Capitalism had indeed seen a vast increase in coal mining and mass car ownership alone. It was growing its use of fossil fuels when it should have been decreasing them.

The nations of the world were caught in a kind of 'tragedy of the commons' where no one wanted to be the first to ease back on polluting the planet – the common, finite land that they all shared.

They UN fudged matters with carbon trading, where the rich could continue to abuse the planet by paying for the privilege. Renewable energy sources such as wind turbines and solar panels were chipping away at the problem but too slowly since governments refused to invest fast enough. It was also rather unfortunate that these clean energy source devices used fossil fuels for their manufacture and transport.

A less spoken matter was the public's involvement. While we kept driving cars and flying on planes, and buying products wrapped in plastic, and buying products of capitalism like garden gnomes that we really, really did not need, we were damaging the planet to produce and transport. We also were guilty in failing to tackle climate change. We too waited for 'someone else' to take action.

The millions of square miles of rainforest burnt and chopped down stuck out like a sore thumb. Plants were the vital sequesters of carbon dioxide from the air. We were severely destabilising the planet to serve the needs and whims of businesses, and the public who continued to consume what the businesses foisted upon them. Unbelievably, the fossil fuel industry were receiving subsidies of $11 million a minute – $5.9 trillion in 2020 alone.

Forest fires and extreme temperatures started to become the norm across the planet. Animal and plant species were being wiped out at the fastest rate the planet had ever witnessed. Yet still no action was being taken as vested interests were too powerful.

Moving past my year of 2021, civil unrest that had started with the likes of the Extinction Rebellion movement grew topsy. It had to because the planet and our species was at stake. The masses grew profoundly disillusioned by the people in power. Countries were signing up to agreements and reneging on them. They were cheating. As soon as one cheated, the whole United Nations concept losses credibility.

In spite of flaring anger at the political and business leader failings and lies, the public needed a more palpable incentive to unite against them en masse. And the increasing numbers of forest fires and extreme temperature events did just that. Third world countries were being told to make climate changes without proper funding while being fried to death by the violent climate.

Mass protests and national strikes kicked in. But what finally had the most telling effect was when those in power were evicted from power. The taboo that we have elected our leaders so must let them lead was so badly compromised now that deposing them became easy. Relatively speaking, that is. They still had to be found and 'extracted' from whichever government or business building they were in.

The police were of course also members of the public. They served to keep the justice but were acutely aware of the failures of government to act on climate change. In Greece, forest fires were destroying homes and government were too slow to preempt and act. Enough police men and women were directly and indirectly affected by these fires to take action. They found it galling that government used them as protection against ever more angry protestors. Rather than listen to the protests, the police were ordered to use rubber bullets, water canons and batons to oppress the protestors. The penny dropped simultaneously one day and the police stopped these oppressions. They downed tools and resumed their normal duties to the deafening cheers by the protestors. Along with some hugs!

Sanctions by government were imposed upon the police as a result. But this of course only served to inflame feelings further. They coordinated in protest. But the law was on their side in a way that it necessarily was not for the public. A second response to systemic government failures finally took place in 2022. It was the pivotal point in the tackling of climate change. It was the catalyst needed to empower the public to start to take over from politicians and business leaders in order to save the planet.

This change in the zeitgeist was almost anti-climatic in nature. A carefully selected group of armed policemen and women walked into the main government building debating chamber, where a very well attended debate was underway. The debate was stopped in its tracks and a hush came over the incumbents. They watched with a mix of bewilderment and curiosity as the police approached the key decision makers in the government. One by one, each was charged with one or more offences of failing to implement climate change policies or fraud or dishonesty in office. Most protested vehemently, but all were handcuffed and lead away. A few opposition party members cheered. Most were stunned, frozen like statues. And of course they could not call on the police to help them out!

These charlatans in public office were in due course taken into law courts, also appropriated by uniformed officers, where they were put on public trial, with the hearings broadcast on social media. This also was a revelation at the time. All except three were convicted and sent to prison.

But this was just the first phase of the planned 'coup'. A carefully selected team of experts in climate, health, education and so on were installed in government in place of the displaced politicians. And proceedings now operated with climate change rather than the economy as the highest priority.

Because this one country showed what was possible, other countries tried and often succeeded in replicating this formerly audacious anarchic behaviour. But many governments were of course now forewarned. And many had far tighter securities, and were happy to deploy the army in defence.

The United Nations surprisingly embraced the earnest focus on climate change. Many commentators in the press at the time suspected that it feared for its continued existence otherwise. But enough National representatives now were seeing the urgency of the need for putting a brake on a climate running rampantly out of control. A sign of the new power the UN wielded took place in the US where Corporations that were suing the government for blocking fossil fuel extraction were told to back off. And they did.

Countries like China, reluctant to reverse fast and vast economic growth that saw a dangerous surge in coal mining and usage, began to see themselves as outliers and at risk of trade sanctions. And eventually, bit by bit, they changed direction.

The United Nations, replete with a swathe of climate, transport, economic and many other International experts now on board, started imposing immediate planet-wide actions. This was in stark and extreme contrast to the decades-long schedule of agreed proposals in past COP meetings that cynically and calculatingly simply served to defer action.

For many, acting decisively now was already too late. But what else could they do but try? And try they did! The nations were collectively put on a kind of war footing – against their ill-practices!

Internationally, production of private use cars was halted. Petrol prices were hiked to prohibitive levels as part of a meaningful pollution tax, the revenues being channeled into manufacture of wind turbines and other clean energy devices. Only vital goods transport was permitted internationally – you holidayed in your own country now. There was public outrage at that, and even more so when bananas and avocados and the like disappeared from many supermarket shelves. Taxes on plastic packaging forced a reversion to paper bags and measurement from containers for many products. Curiously enough, the public liked this return to times of interaction with shop staff.

Intensive farming that was destroying the soils was outlawed. Animal foodstuffs were taxed heavily, needed when methane from cattle was a huge warming factor. Thousands of peat bogs to decarbonise the air were created. Deforestation was stopped instantly, with funding giving in lieu to those who had only resorted to tree felling as a desperate means to making a living.

The world was thrown into a deep state of shock for these and other changes were as profound as they were immediate – at least mostly, because some nations still dragged their heels. The UN swiftly supplied the sticks and carrots to change their attitudes.

Free solar heating, and free double and triple glazing and other home insulation tempered public outrage. To a degree.

It took a while for the changes to bed in and become accepted, but an intense climate action promotional media campaign did normalise the changes. Many were galvanised in a war spirit to 'do their bit'. Many saw it prudent and practical to start growing their own food. Especially when it was explained in no uncertain terms that food waste was not only a gigantic criminal waste in the West in a world where many eat too little, but that reducing waste was the biggest way for the public to lower emissions. Nation states, steered in humane rather than wealth-gathering ways helped on this front by razing obsolete Commercial plots to the ground and converting them into communal allotments. Some roads no longer carrying cars were even bulldozed up and grassed over, with vegetable beds installed along the centre.

I was beginning to see how the world had evolved to the state it was now in. I had not finished this first book, but it was getting late so I turned in for the night, my mind dancing with thoughts.

Each day made this 'hallucination' ever more real and ever less a fabrication of my mind. Sleep had been fractured by sheer excitement about the history of my former future, if I can describe it that way. I desperately wanted to read on, especially in the second book about post climate crisis evolution, but had another meeting with Brian. Maybe that would provide an opportunity to get his take on that evolution history. If anyone could, a historian could.

I was able to make my own way this time as Eric had some chores to attend to, although he did not use that word. For him, these were vital life-affirming activities, even if dull to my senses. Brian had scheduled a stretch of four hours to meet with me, spanning lunch. He was as cheerful and bright-eyed as I was dull of look and mind. But my slumbering mind was soon awakened when I asked Brian to start with a potted history of the time following the slow but eventually effective reversal of climate change. I did not, however, expect him to launch into a narrative about human nature.

"There is something almost charmingly naïve about the self-importance of the human race in the first two centuries of the third millennium." were his opening words.

I flinched in defence of my era. With a moment to ponder as he awaited the impact of his words, I decided to operate as a blank and non-judgemental slate for all that he said. Absorb now, critique later. He continued :

"They presumed that their technological prowess represented a kind of human evolutionary peak. There was a casual presumption that they had evolved beyond all of their predecessors. This mirrored earlier centuries when lands were invaded by 'civilised' people who arrogantly presumed themselves to be superior to the indigenous tribes that they encountered. They were seen as barbaric simpletons who should be destroyed or forced to adopt the values and life-styles of the invaders. No effort was made to understand the delicate harmony with which many such peoples lived in balance with nature. They did not see that these were in fact superior life-styles, even if just in the absence of the explosive, insensitive expansion that saw the rest of us nearly destroy the planet."

"I am entirely in agreement with you here. It has always galled me that dominion over others was so prevalent in the past and just took a different form over the centuries." I replied. He nodded with a smile and continued :

"Like all other living beings, humans evolve in fits and starts, essentially adapting to the environment rather than to some plan of advancement. This should be clear in reflection when pondering past civilisations. Many of these reached peaks and supplied intellectual foundations for our modern 'superior' life.

Humans in the early part of the third millennium were actually regressing, in fact, lazily dependent on these inheritances and newly evolved technological 'crutches'. Mobile phones supplied so very much that young people were losing the ability to actually read books. They were being spoilt rather than being advanced by technology.

Even if humans at that time had reached an evolutionary pinnacle, it was not one to proclaim with joy. People still lied to and deceived others on a regular basis – much more so with social media anonymity, absent the vital face to face interaction cues. Wars still rumbled on. The inequality between the haves and have-nots was vast and accelerating, with half the human population in poverty. These were very much not Utopian times.

When books sought to portray Utopias, they tended to focus on environmental idealism along with some cultural changes. Rarely did they envisage human evolution as an additional factor that was needed for any hope of a viable form of moderately Utopian life. It reminds me of the psychological notion that you may go on holiday to some tropical paradise, but you never get away from yourself.

Maybe it is because evolution is seen as a mostly painfully slow and fraught matter that it is not factored in. We assumed humans as we were then, without change, could be viable occupants of a Utopian land."

I was intrigued. And thirsty. So we wandered off to the cafe to get some herbal tea, along with some nibbles that were new to me. A taste that was hard to describe, much as it is hard to relate the taste of a passion fruit. Maybe. Anyway, it had an earthy taste, presumably like truffles. I asked Brian why he was talking about Utopian lives. I was interested in the actual evolution of life that had taken place post-apocalypse. He explained that the seismic changes that were needed to over climate change had cultivated a world-wide reflection on the direction we humans should be headed in. Should we return to life as before, but in a more tempered fashion. Or would it be far better to rethink, to re-envisage. To re-engineer societies. And many naturally turned to books on Utopian futures, seen as excellent catalysts for re-imagining life on the planet. Countless ideas were expounded. Much argument ensued. The United Nations got embroiled in some of the discussions. It may have started in a confused mess, but it had precious momentum. Too many people wanted change, not least the avoidance of power-mongering by governments and corporations.

And in the centuries that followed, humans did indeed evolve. This happened in part because they were violently forced to adapt by the climate change that fried and swamped their original habits. The many changes compounded to have a transformational effect on human nature, and most of all on how humans interacted with each other. It is hard to underestimate human relationships. They are a key measure of our species evolutionary progress. Even in the early third millennium, we were social creatures in ways that transcended all other living beings. We cared for each other and gained so splendidly from the synergy of collaborating collectives. When humans worked well together, we were indeed much more than the sum of our number.

But we were still plagued by inter-relationship troubles. Many did not realise that as a species, we were at a kind of half-way point. Half-way between the selfish, egocentric nature of our primate ancestors and fluid, trouble-free occupants of future societies or Utopias.

The forces of self-preservation at the time acted as dangerous undercurrents in our interactions with others. Forces that used emotions that were hard to resist, such as the gnawing desire to seek revenge when cheated by another. Those that cheated were bypassing societal rules to lazily acquire what they needed or wanted, so punishment was often sought. Conflict, even unspoken, was regularly present. Too often, humans simply annoyed each other, even in trivial ways. Telling someone that their hair was a bit of a mess would ruffle feathers, even if the person was quite aware of the reality of this fact.

There were, however, signs of individual evolution that sought for the release from the gravity and gravitas of an emotionally driven life. Mindfulness allowed practitioners to pause before becoming beholden to the emotions that were springing up throughout each day. To see if the narrative attached to these emotions, such as the desire for revenge, were indeed worth heeding. These people started challenging and changing automatic behaviours. Their mindfulness broke them free from autopilot lives.

Some cultures, such as in the Nordic countries like Denmark, were very much evolved beyond this mid-point. This was most notably the case if you compared them with warring nations like the US that sought to sate its seemingly endless need for petrol for gas-guzzling cars by invading oil-rich nations.

East Asian countries like Japan had evolved beyond the mid-point between self and other collectivism. Relationships between people were pivotal, often surpassing concerns about individuals. People accommodated others in ways that humans in the West were less likely to do, where the self was more the focus. But Japan suffered with too much suppression of the individual – loss of face in society sometimes even lead to suicide.

However, individual and cultural change was never going to move the human race to the end point of effortless social interaction. The primate forces of the time were simply too dominant to placate. Additionally, the tiny capacity of human consciousness sorely limited abilities to manage these forces in addition to the interaction efforts themselves. So we ended up with mass levels of social anxiety, where people struggled to cope with the demands of interaction with other humans who were also driven by powerful personal forces and who also lacked conscious capacity to cope with much friction.

You might wonder why I refer to the power of consciousness as tiny. In that mid-point evolutionary period, humans could only ever pay full attention to one matter at a time. And that ability was demanding to sustain. Both the effort of doing so, and the additional effort needed to avoid distractions was swiftly draining for many humans.

In short, our conscious mind was stupendously and crazily under-powered and under-resourced. The visual cortex of the brain could handle a vast parallel stream of signals from the eyes, and generate a real-time 'movie' of the world around us, but our conscious mind could only pay attention to a tiny part of that at any one time. Some disputed that limitation, especially busy mothers, who claimed that they frequently multi-tasked. There is no denying that child-care seemed to demand that. But it was not possible to pay full conscious attention to each task. You could focus on a TV programme while stirring food, or the other way round. But not pay full attention to both. And that single-threaded attention would readily become disturbed by screams from a distraught child ...

Quite why the poverty of conscious mind power had gotten humans as far as they had is itself quite a matter for reflection and wonder. It would be near impossible for a human from this time period to explain how a truly multi-tasking conscious mind might feel. They were so accustomed to jumping fast from one matter to the next that they presumed they were multi-tasking. They could not imagine fully attending to a conversation with their friend as well as fully attending to the man at the bar who was talking too loud but on an interesting subject.

The brain was always able, in principle, to support this parallelism, except of course that we can even now only talk in a single threaded manner. And we can only look at one person or object at a time that we are attending to. But the ability to listen attentively to more than one person speaking at a time is extremely empowering. To be able to take a message in the ear from your secretary while in a meeting and yet not miss anything said is very valuable."

It was at this point that I asked him to pause there because something had clicked in my mind. I recalled the puzzlement in my mind when Ana had behaved so maturely. No, it was not that, but what happened when her mother spoke at the dinner table. In hindsight, she most certainly seemed to have this faculty of listening attentively to more than one conversation at a time. Quite remarkable.

"But how do you instigate this massive change in consciousness? I am deeply intrigued as I saw Eric's daughter behave as if she had this ability." I asked of Brian.

"Truth be told, I am disappointed to tell, we did not instigate the change. It just evolved over the centuries. It might even have originally evolved in response to the need to track many threads of social media chat. Also, radical changes in diet and subtle changes to our digestive systems and metabolisms saw a greater flow of energy to our brains. In the past, the brain was deemed by evolution to be too energy hungry. Survival of body was still deemed more vital than cognitive power, so the brain was ever focused on economy of energy use. But the general rise in energy allowed a less frugal mind to evolve.

The change was akin to the greater attention capability of long term meditators who tend to hear with greater attention than mere mortals. Kim Peeks, a gifted 'idiot savant' in the twentieth century was purportedly able to read two pages of a book simultaneously. Now these abilities had become commonplace. And the notion of only being able to focus on one thing at a time now seems like a bad handicap. The energy needed was actually reduced in one sense because a calm mind that can deal with multiple threads of information without being overloaded is less energy hungry.

Those who were originally blessed with the faculty to fully attend to more than one matter at a time tended to reproduce more in part because of the attractiveness of the combination of calm and the capacity to attend to internal thoughts and what others were saying to them simultaneously.

The loss of irritation that resulted is a sign of the far greater tolerance of others that evolved. A kind of automatic mindfulness also replaced the automatic enactment of emotional urges that beset humans in the past. Now, emotions are less potent, less insistent. Being 'chilled' is now the widespread nature of humans.

In our ancestors, the repeated engagement of strong emotions had an accumulative wearing and conditioning effect on the central nervous system. They were often battered and bruised by emotions. Many developed mental health difficulties, such as the aforementioned social anxiety, where a nervousness about how well they harmonised with others was amplified. To confound matters, that anxious state was then attacked as a weakness. A kind of awful catch-22."

I listened in rapt awe. That all this could take place over a matter of centuries seemed implausible. But I only had to reflect on my own history to see how barbaric and untrusting humans were to each other as a general matter just a few centuries before my era. We were indeed 'domesticating' ourselves.

Humans had domesticated cats and dogs and farm animals over a similar time period. So it did seem viable. But was Brian hiding at least some 'master-race' eugenics programme that was involved in such a radical change? Was it all simply adaption to change? I would hear him out and ponder on this matter later. He continued :

"In spite of this evolution of capability, the simple matter of mixing with other humans remains a tricky matter. We know not what goes on in the heads of others unless they reveal it to us. In past times, this was endlessly exploited. Humans lied to and deceived others to smooth social situations but also to exploit the invisibility of their thoughts.

Humans have different interests, understandings, morals, ethics, beliefs and feelings. In our early days as a species, encounters with 'strangers' tended to result in fight or flight or sexual engagement. By the time of your days, we had advanced spectacularly to be able to live in big cities where we might pass by hundreds of strangers on a daily basis and yet feel generally fairly safe (although the context is King here). This is a tribute to both the evolution of our brains and of the accompanying culture. In societies riven by crime or violence or caught up in wars, this was not the case. But most cultures taught the value of cooperation and respect for others.

But our brains had evolved also. We learnt to tolerate others. To be relatively comfortable in the presence of many unknown to us. But evolution chose a compromise to achieve this. We retained many of our primate instincts, but layered on top, in the vast frontal cortex of the brain was the seat of reason that provided override and tempering mechanisms for these instincts. So we did not seek to kill someone just because they accidentally bumped into us on the pavement. Mostly. We generally suppressed such primal instincts.

But this patching mechanism created a swathe of problems. The act of suppression itself was painful for some both in the short term and long. Not being able to express ourselves, even if barbarically so, was caustic. It cloyed at us. And it festered, leaving us mentally scarred.

Alcohol exposed this problem. Often painfully. It removed some of these inhibitions so that our more primal natures could express themselves. Alcohol was not the real problem – what it revealed was.

A more effective and less primal and reactive relationship evolved between the frontal cortex and the Amygdala – the emotion centre of the brain. It was hard to be sure if mindfulness was cause or consequence. Essentially, an integrated thought and emotion responsiveness replaced the raw emotional reactivity that drove much human behaviour. Thought and emotion were bed fellows rather than competing forces.

The original calmness of the Nordic countries became a global norm. Anger did not flair into unreasonable aggression, but remained a force for correcting injustices in a confrontational but reasonable way. The counterpoint to this was a calmer, more thoughtful acceptance of wrongdoing."

This certainly sounded very Utopian. Highly desirable but surely it could not really take hold across the planet? There must be factions stubbornly resistant to or genetically devoid of such change? Would there not be people taking advantage of the goodness of others?

As before, I reflected and pondered the shopping street near my house. How many thousands of times I had walked along with no fear at all for being attacked, even absent any police to regulate the public. Most people had already evolved to be nice in public. Now the niceties were becoming entrenched in more moments in life. Brian continued, explaining that it was a state of evolution, not a wondrous peak :

"As admitted earlier, however, there remain inherent difficulties in human interactions. This is unavoidable to a large degree because of the vast complexity and variability of human natures. So you are right to ask how a brain that lacks inhibition handles irritations and conflicts. At root, the key is near universal mindfulness, where a Stoic pause allows reason to handle tricky situations where in the past emotions bulldozed in with great speed. Additionally, in arguments or discussions, emotions used to narrow or polarise opinion. Now, not only is the emotional engagement much more tempered, but the mind can comfortably fully attend to our own opinion and that of the person we are talking with. There is no vying for attention, so we can give full merit to both viewpoints – in parallel!

And as an aside, in games like Go, we can naturally see the detail of a fighting sequence whilst simultaneously being fully aware of the effect of that fight on the rest of the board. We see context and detail in parallel to enormous benefit.

Before all this, a major affliction of humans at that mid-way point you have experienced was a forcefulness of the subconscious mind upon the conscious mind. Those who tried to meditate in that era found that the subconscious mind 'chatter' was relentless. No matter how much they calmed their mind, no matter how much they avoided buying into the chatter, it persisted. Practitioners would be bombarded by ruminations about the past, concerns about the present and projections and forecasts about the future. When meditating they were trying to be a human 'being' yet the subconscious always wanted you to be a human 'doing', always attending to the needs and wants of daily life.

This near-ceaseless bombardment acted in a statistical manner, operating on the basis that the more frequently and intensely it would urge you to take action, the more likely that you would so. The subconscious could not demand, but merely nag, repeatedly. That was a kind of price humans paid for a degree of conscious autonomy. But if someone noticed carefully, even when they acceded to a demand, and planned to do something about it, until that plan was enacted, the urging words would persist. So it stopped being a rational force. Merely a burdensome one and a blunt one that used repetition to coerce.

Meditation allowed some respite from that, but few were able to master that skill. These days, a meditative state is an effortless one. The mind can disengage the chatter at will. No longer are you a kind of hamster on a treadwheel, but more in control of your destiny.

This same dominant and relentless emotion/narrative combination force was seen in other ways. For example, the emotional and physical urge to urinate was and is a prudent one. But the urge to have sex when the chance of coupling was extraordinarily remote was an extreme and dominant force. Whilst we should feel some compunction to seek a mate in order to procreate, to propagate our genes, it the urges were pretty relentless. And one that was also frequently very misguided. So it was crude of force by repetition but also easily confused in direction or outcome.

My favourite example was the proliferation of pornography in that mid-point era. That a moving or still image of a naked or semi-clad human could arouse another was an indication of the extremeness of the 'opportunist' sex-drive. The slightest hint that coupling might be possible was enough to sexually arouse someone, even though celluloid or paper was very much not human, nor might lead to the humans portrayed being available to you.

So the force was nearly entirely primitive and divorced from the rational mind. And when a chance encounter with a real human lead to intercourse, the rational mind was swamped out of the reckoning by sexual opportunist forces that tended to blind the engaged couple to thoughts of a lifetime caring for offspring.

The cost and sheer duration of parenting really should have called for a more rational influence upon the sex-drive, one that did much later arrive as a corollary of the better coordination of front and hind brain systems.

More exciting and more radical even that this was that we evolved a tangible dialogue between the conscious mind and the subconscious mind. It was no longer madness to talk to oneself! We could now have a say in subconscious processes. There is far too much to say about this right now, but as a taster, imagine being able to ask the subconscious to disengage thinking so that we can sleep. To even be able to break depression loops by telling the subconscious that it is in a self-defeating spin? To negotiate with the subconscious on what were automatic but crude mechanisms. Like confirming a dental appointment so that it could lower the pain level rather than inflict us with pain unnecessarily.

Many mental health issues now failed to materialise in part from this new faculty and in part from the true ability to multi-task. But also because we could now actually ask the subconscious about reasons for decisions made. To ask why we are fearful starting the new job we so desperately wanted to have. And to thereby learn that in our childhood we were conditioned into believing that we should not harbour ambitions. We can ask of the subconscious mind that it focusses most of its attention on a problem that is now most urgent. Can you imagine how different life is now with this interface now opened? No longer are we blindly subjected to buried decisions. We have a say in matters. With our own minds! As if that was actually radical in the first place.

There was another relic from our early ancestors. Greed. Those that erred on the side of acquiring more than they needed tended to out-survive those that did not. Greed was originally for food, shelter and mates. But eventually it became greed of money and power. Our minds seemed to compare our wealth this week with last week, and to seek more if we are less endowed. The mind worked more on novelty – change – than absolutes. So no matter how wealthy someone became, there was an aversion to loss and a clamour for more.

A strange peculiarity of man's past was the matter of pain. It had been presumed that it signalled the status of injury or infection. Yet the level and nature of pain was a calculation by the brain as to the level of *protection* the body needed. As the site healed, the brain could get lazy in checking that status and inappropriately continue to produce pain. So here we have another emotional system that was not serving us well. It too changed over time to more tightly couple site healing status with pain level.

All these changes to human brains operated in parallel with cultural changes. They fed back to each other, compounding their mutual effect.

The placating of insatiable greed, for example, fitted in with more egalitarian and equitable societies – endless wealth accumulation was no longer a force and taught as unattractive. Capitalism changed gradually to serve customers and respect the environment, with profit no longer the focal point, until the provision of needs rather than wealth accumulation was restored.

These societies that promoted and favoured the collective and collaboration without denying opportunities for individual expression, achievement and reward also tackled a major issue at the mid-way point. The matter of individual status or reputation. Humans used to lie and deceive to protect and bolster their standing. Absent inhibitions, they needed support for their reputation to avoid a regression to deceptive practices. The collective had to grow tolerance for failure, weakness, adversity and of course vast differences in human natures and potentials to avoid the problems that came with reputation cultivation and protection.

There was a strange consequence to the cohesive and egalitarian life style that evolved. The level at which humans competed against each other reduced significantly. Sport became less partisan, the games more important than the results. There was some yearning for that fighting spirit to manifest itself in all its 'glory' once again, but this was seen as a small price to pay."

Phew, I thought! What a lot to take in, but so mesmerising that I sat there absorbed like a child in a sweet shop with a fistful of coins. Not that I could or should have suspected anything less over a period of centuries. But it was starkly painful to realise, by comparison, how the people off my time were (or are?) primitive and under-developed, easily triggered into inappropriate and costly behaviours.

I thanked him profoundly for all this new information as we set off for lunch. But I called the meeting short at that point as there was already far too much to reflect upon.

Before we parted, Brian made a surprise suggestion. He had spoken with Eric and they had both agreed that he should experience more fully social life here. It was fine and dandy to mix with a few people and sit in a simple academic eating area, but to more fully experience the nature of these evolved people, he said that I should mix with a mass of them.

When I asked if that meant a trip to a shopping centre, eyebrows were raised. Clearly, it now transpired, that these were relics of my 'past'. No 'high street'. No shopping malls or arcades. Instead, I was to attend a music concert in three days time! Now that would be most exciting!

In the meantime, I was to help *and relax* at the 'allotment' each morning, and read in the afternoons. I was also supremely pleased to discover that Eric had a Go board and was a decent player. Not only that, but a very deep one with slate and shell stones. So I was to intersperse my reading with the odd game of Go with both Eric and Ana.

I swiftly completed the climate change book, far too impatient to wait a moment longer to embrace and devour the book on the revolutions in lifestyle and leadership that swept across the planet. I had been given a delicious taster and now wanted to flesh that out.

And I discovered that I was indeed correct in presuming human intervention on our evolution. There appears to have been a series of thinly concealed eugenics programmes, operating under the guise of 'domesticating and enhancing humans'. I was not sure if even that disguised descriptor could have been well received either. A key thrust was to isolate the kinds of people who had driven the world to a near fatal demise. The psychopaths. The greedy. The brutal. But not to imprison them but to actually give them a good secure healthy life in their own communities in villages and towns separated from the rest of the people. Much as when convicts were evicted and transported from Britain to Australia.

It seemed at least partially very controlling and heartless. Sure, these were tough people entirely oblivious to the harm their own interests inflicted upon others. Now they had to co-exist will like-natured people. And they surprisingly did, prevailing in relative luxury supplied by the state, which heavily constrained these people to these communities.

Were the rest of the public angry at such pampering of outcasts? Not really, it seemed, since education on such social matters and the logistics of handling miscreants was part of everyone's upbringing. They were happy to toil to supply the needs to be separated from them.

Freed from the kinds of characters that abused power, the rest of the people were able to be lead with surety that their interests were always ahead of possible personal gain by those who lead. But they had learnt not to trust that power would be handled unselfishly as it always seemed to corrupt many, intoxicating them so that abuse of power was too attractive for some. So it took a great length of time before leaders were again trusted.

The net effect over the centuries of a more egalitarian life was profound.

Whilst reading, it occurred to me that in case I should suddenly disappear – that this hallucination should vanish and I awaken back in my own 'dark ages' – that I should try to find some way of verifying the authenticity of my current experience. To find some media of my era, if somehow possible, to see if things do indeed evolve according to this 'hallucination'. So I asked Brian if I could revisit the academic library. He said in reply that there was an online system that I could use.

I found my own way there later that day. 'Sevenday' they called it. 'Eightday' was when we were to travel to that much anticipated pop concert. But I never did make it. I never did get to experience mingling with excited concert goers who had a calm nature. I was wondering how that nature and exciting events married together.

I will explain what happened. A friendly lady who was clearly a 'worker' at this faculty took me to a room with angled desks. They were at near head height when you sat down in z-shaped chairs. These angled your legs to limit the load on your spine. We had them in my time but here they were deployed to good effect when sustained concentration might otherwise have been injurious to the body. The chair buzzed after 20 minutes, the screen faded and I was asked to walk around a little to stretch my legs. How cool was that!

I duly obliged and resumed the process of familiarisation with this modern day 'internet'. It was surprisingly similar to what I had become used to, but was entirely free from advertisements. This accorded with the culture of sharing and the absence of work. No work, no products to promote, I guess. Yet I was using a product. A powerful screen-based system. Maybe state produced.

I found an archive of British newspapers dating back to the early 2000's. I found the paper for the day before my 'hallucination'. It seemed, as expected, entirely plausible, even down to the sports results. This hallucination was nothing if not coherent and believable. It was when I moved to the next day that it happened. Reading ahead to the future after the time I 'departed' started to make me felt dizzy. I was unsure why. I skipped a few weeks to see what might be happening in my immediate future. What caught my eye before I passed out was the invasion into the Cop27 climate change conference by protestors. They took to the microphones and declared the delegates here to be enacting crimes of passivity against the planet. They handcuffed them and barricaded the doors to block access by the police. They demanded action of these bewildered decision makers.

And that was all I was able to absorb.

With a brutal shock to my senses, I found myself back in the laboratory. Back in my own time. Maybe I was entitled to know about the far future, when I would not be around to experience it. That something too close to my time posed some kind of risk to this exposure to the future. Yet it felt far too tangible to be an hallucination.

I sat quite deflated. I discovered that almost no time had elapsed. In response to questions asked of me, I kept my experience to myself. I concocted some plausible bright lights stories to tell and made my way home.

As you will have guessed, a few weeks later, the Cop27 conference was duly invaded by protestors. The newspaper I had read in 'the future' was identical to the copy I now held in my hands. It seemed that my future would pan out better than many climate change fear-mongers were proclaiming. But I felt sad knowing that the humans of my time had so much growing up to do.

Shallow thinking

It is so easy to fall prey to blinkered thinking

Life gets pretty complicated for most of us. There is often too much to do in too little time. So we have evolved mechanisms that prune a lot of unnecessary things away. By way of example, the information from our senses is heavily filtered by our brains to present what is most pertinent at any one moment (although conditions such as autism and schizophrenia offer evidence of reduced filtering).

When we are in a crowd of people, we do not need to know the hair colour, clothing choices, and a myriad of other details about these people. We are just in a crowd. We may choose to focus in on someone who catches our eye, but in general, our minds are more attuned to our shopping list, or other matters. So there is a distinct limit to our depth of thinking and awareness. We can and do often think shallowly. We do so for good reason since our brain has a lot to do and is expensive to operate, so it tends to err on the side of economy, as already explained.

However, this economising can create a premature horizon to our thinking beyond which there often lies a very different truth to the one we perceive. By way of a trivial example, we may tell someone that they look beautiful today, and fail to realise that this implies that the person was not appealing the last time we saw them when we did not comment.

You may have a tendency to invariably stick with the first thing that comes to mind in a situation. This *einstellung* effect stops your mind looking beyond the obvious on the assumption that the obvious will always be the best. This stymies further and deeper thinking.

As the mindfulness chapter will later discuss, by pausing to look beyond our immediate gut reaction to situations, more subtle aspects will start to reveal themselves. You may, for example, have a gut reaction that psychedelic drugs are dangerous. This reaction puts a brake on further exploration. If you were to inquire deeper, you might learn that they have been shown to help terminal cancer patients face death without fear, for example. Our shallowness of thought creates a shallowness of inquiry.

William Deresiewicz made this general observation of shallow thinking :

> "I find for myself that my first thought is never my best thought. My first thought is always someone else's; it's always what I've already heard about the subject, always the conventional wisdom."

I will illustrate shallow thinking with some short examples.

McDonalds advertisements

McDonald's food adverts clearly show very generous, perfectly crafted burgers, such as you are unlikely to be served. So a more aggrieved member of the public might feel it appropriate to sue them for misrepresentation. But think just a little further, and you can see that the error might be with the McDonalds restaurant they visited that was serving smaller, imperfect burgers, rather than a fault of the adverts. They may be failing to adhere to their franchise demands. If you wanted to persist in suing McDonald's you might feel that you would need to eat meals at enough branches to build a statistical case. Further exploration, however, might make you discover that the franchises are supplied with a regulated and standardised supply of burger patties from McDonald's. So you may have a case against the advert courtesy of one restaurant visit after all. In this example, you can see that more thinking happens as a consequence of keeping an inquiring, questioning mind.

Calories in, calories out

The diet mantra that it is all a matter of 'calories in, calories out' is a beautiful example of shallow, simplistic thinking because it appeals to our economic mind. It makes sufficient, superficial common sense that we tend to feel no need to think further. As the first line of defence, proponents of the mantra even cite the first law of thermodynamics to defend the view that we can only lose weight if we consume less than we use. (Except that the human body is an open system, and therefore not itself subject to that law).

The thinking person's approach to this matter might be to read and learn that the calorific measure of food energy is based on the literal burning of food. Our bodies, however, do not process food by burning it. So we observe the first nuance. Carbohydrates elevate insulin levels, and fats do not. These lead to different metabolic states. The consequence is that the same calorific value will have different effects on the body and metabolism, the second nuance.

There is also the presumption that we can readily accompany reduced calorie intake with increased exercise – as if the former would not affect the latter. When you eat less food, however, the amount of energy available for you to expend is reduced since the body starts to preserve it, the third nuance. The simplistic calories in, calories out thinking here conveniently ignores body dynamics and metabolism.

Heart measurements

It is recommended that you exercise for 20-25 minutes per day with a heart rate in the range of 55-85% of your maximum heart rate, which is calculated as 220 minus your age. If you are 60, your maximum heart rate will be given as 160 b.p.m., but if you have a resting heart rate of 80 b.p.m., you will enter that range by raising it by only 8 beats – a mere 10% rise. This would likely be achieved by the simple act of standing up.

Did no one think about factoring in that resting heart rate? Someone with an 80 b.p.m. resting heart rate will have low blood pumping volume. By contrast, a low resting heart rate of say 50 b.p.m. would indicate a heart that pumps a large amount of blood each stroke. Elevating it to 88 b.pm. would be a rise of 76% and thereby would be working it hard. Be wary of simplistic calculations such as this offered as 'standards'. Thinking can lead you to find a better way by asking a qualified physician or trainer to *dynamically* determine your optimal safe exercising heart rate range.

Supraventricular tachycardia is a condition where your heart suddenly beats much faster than normal, as mine did on a number of nights in bed recently. It disturbed me enough to seek advice from my doctor. The guidance she received and offered to me was that this condition has a threshold of 100 b.p.m.. You can hopefully see where I am going with this. Once again, even with critical matters such as potential heart disorders, we see an unchallenged simplicity. The figure is the high end of the 60 b.p.m. to 100 b.p.m. range of normal resting heart rates. Rather than determine a value unique to the person being evaluated according to *their* resting heart rate, a lazy single figure is used to determine a universal threshold.

Have a go yourself at seeing where thinking can expose simple metrics by looking at the Body Mass Index (BMI). It is defined as the body mass in kilograms divided by the square of the body height in metres. What is missing here? Is it a meaningful measure?

Accessing my web site files

When I recently tried to edit a page on my website I received a message with a code stating that the access had timed out. So I contacted the help desk who eventually told me that I had exceeded my site file storage limit because a log file of site system messages had grown too big. They said that it was this limit that was bizarrely preventing site access.

I thought about what was happening here, not least the vast amount of time it took for them to discover the cause of my problem. First, this was likely to be a common problem as log files necessarily do fill up unless purged. So why was this common occurrence not recorded for frontline staff to suggest as a first port of call? Second, why did this log file capacity problem not trigger the technical department to develop a solution where the log file was periodically split when reaching a certain size, with older, obsolete log entries purged? Third, why was a 'file full error' message not passed back to my web file access program as the problem cause instead of an 'access denied' message? These are examples of problems that get repeated endlessly because no one is thinking often enough about how things could be better.

Toyota adopted the concept of **kaizen** in their car production lines – both a process and, vitally, an attitude of continuous improvement. Anyone could stop the production line to signal even a small problem. That problem would then be explored as far back as necessary to determine the cause. For example, a part discovered to be made out of tolerance might be traced back to confusing instructions for the machine making it. Only seasoned workers could work around this flaw – a new worker was confused and made the part defectively. Error causal analysis and action is used by Toyota to prevent repeats of such errors.

When the Americans tried to clone kaizen and the 'Lean production' methodology (that Toyota had taken a full two decades to perfect) they struggled to let go of their hierarchical management structures. In such controlling rather than delegating company structures, matters of production line stoppages are deemed a high management concern. So they denied the production line workers autonomy to act on problems by stopping the line, and in one fell swoop started undermining the kaizen methods and ethos. Likewise, effort into problem causal analysis by the Americans was implemented only in proportion to the perceived scale of the problem. The Japanese, however, gained a great deal more by tracing back even minor issues to their root cause because a tiny symptom may not be caused by a tiny problem. Moreover, minor problems can be more likely to recur.

Medical drugs

Bringing a medical drug to market is an extraordinarily long and expensive process. It involves patient trials that operate via a 'double- blind' protocol where neither trial administrators nor patients know whether the drug or an inert placebo is administered. A drug will be approved when there is clear evidence that a sufficient number of trial patients benefited from it, and the 'side-effects' did not outweigh the benefits.

If you think about what this means, you will realise that the drug you are about to take for your condition might have failed to work for some of the trial patients. And that for some of these, it may have set their recovery back somewhat. So an 'approved' drug is only statistically effective. You will not know in advance if it will work for or against you.

By way of example, the well established pain relief drug morphine is known to have adverse effects on some patients. So the common thinking that an approved drug is somehow certified in a water-tight fashion is one to avoid.

Homeless people

When we see a homeless person asking for money at the side of the street, we may hear a voice in our head that urges us not to proffer money fearing they will waste it on drink or drugs. If we are to think about why our instinct should be this way inclined, we can realise that we have effectively been subjected to indoctrinating, normalising thought patterns. We are conditioned into seeing homelessness as a failure of self, and that those too weak to overcome this plight would prefer to indulge in an alcohol-induced stupor rather than seek an escape to a better life.

No doubt this is the case for some. But not all. Some people lose their job and then their home in quick succession, the latter conditional on the former. To add insult to injury, their family can snub them, the life- line they then clearly desperately need now removed. The craving for drugs is often a craving for a temporary escape from the barbarity of sleeping rough – a brief dissolution of pain and discomfort.

Some homeless people I have spoken with carry scars where they have been kicked, punched and urinated upon for the 'crime' of being destitute. The homeless are sadly seen as an easy target for alcohol- induced inhibition in night clubbers – those who *do* have a home to go to and who are the ones more clearly abusing drugs than the homeless.

Childhood obesity

We are told, by way of a starter, that childhood obesity can be tackled with the two simple measures of exercising more eating less. When we think more, however, we start to see that these are just two starting points. We additionally need to look at *why* children do not exercise as much as before, and *why* they now overeat.

When we look back a few decades, we see slimmer children were the norm, and that it was the *nature* of their exercise that was the crucial factor. When children roamed in woods and fields near their houses, they spent hours so engrossed that they often forgot to eat. Since blood mostly diverted away from their stomachs, it would be less likely that the body would remind them to eat either. In modern times, when children sit passively at home using electronic devices for entertainment, it is too easy for them to graze on food, in spite of necessarily much-reduced energy needs.

Door handles

Many shop doors have pull handles on both sides. Yet they only open one way. You must push the 'pull' handle to enter the shop and pull the other pull handle to exit the shop. Why is this the case?

The outside pull handle is used – once a day – to pull the door shut when locking up. It is then pulled by mistake countless times by customers. Why did the door designer not think to leave the outside as a plate to push and recess a closing door handle at the top or the bottom of the door? It does not have to be overly easy for the shop worker to pull the door closed as it is just a once a day event. Alternatively, maybe the designers could even find a way of hiding the pull handle behind the push plate. The public pays a disproportionate penalty on countless days for a lack of thinking by the door designers (maybe also a lack of thinking on the part of shop owners who do not feed this problem back to the manufacturers).

Creative and lateral thinking

Vital skills that too many schools suppress ...

No single way of thinking applies to all situations. The applications of thought needed to remove a rusted screw in a machine is entirely different to that required to solve algebraic equations, or that needed to supply the defusing words that are essential to help calm down a heated debate between two people.

School tends to force linear, logical, *convergent* thinking onto us, with the consequence that *divergent* thinking all too often becomes marginalised. As a consequence, *creativity* that stems from, and is fuelled by divergent thinking becomes a casualty of this strait-jacket attitude. The reality is that our brains supply us with both convergent and divergent thinking abilities – they are equally inherent and natural for us if given a chance, but the odds are stacked against the latter in most schools.

Creative thinking marries poorly with school curricula, which is determined in large part by academically-minded politicians who decree unbalanced school agendas. It is marginalised as a 'touchy-feely' part of the arts, a domain also seen as unimportant. Yet creativity is increasingly valuable in business, where innovation is often a foundation of success or the means of recovery from hard times.

Psychotherapists, for example, need to be able to tackle patient problems from many angles. They use creativity to reframe the patient plight in ways that create an epiphany where the penny drops and the mental trap is unlocked. When does our education system intentionally cultivate that type of thinking?

You can get a sense of the constraining nature of the convergent thinking the education system conditions into us with a classic problem. You are asked how many matches would get played in a knockout tennis tournament that has a field of 48 players. Immediately, your mind can sense difficulty because fields usually have 32, 64 or 128 players – numbers that are a power of 2. So you might start to map out how you would insert byes in the first round, and then see how the other rounds pan out. Then count the matches to be played.

Instead, however, you might think laterally and see from a broader perspective – that only the event winner will not lose a match, and everyone else will lose a match. From a field of 48 players, there will therefore be 47 losers. Every match yields one loser, so there will be 47 matches. It really is that simple. Linear, convergent conditioning may have made you feel uncomfortable with such a calculation. It seems implausibly simple. Can you instinctively trust it? If not, then you may have a lot to gain by acquiring a better balance in your life between convergent and divergent thinking.

Knowledge can constrain

I will use an example from the Internet to illustrate the nature of lateral thinking. It will show how 'obvious' constraints in a situation tend to blind linear thinkers to the path to the best solution to a problem. The prominent features of a problem create a kind of gravity that draws you into retaining them at the forefront of your mind. This gravity theme rears its head again.

A man interviewed for a job was given a fictional and somewhat artificial scenario where he was driving past a bus stop where three people were sitting in shelter from the rain. The girl of his dreams, an old friend who had saved his life in the past, and an old lady desperately in need of medical attention. He is told that his car has one spare seat (they did not point out that this would, therefore, be a tiny car). He was asked to whom he would give a lift. Think about this a while before reading on.

His smart answer was to give the car keys to his friend to take the old lady to hospital, allowing himself the opportunity to sit alone with the girl of his dreams at the bus stop, thereby getting to know her.

This is clearly a contrived situation, but the moot point here is that the mind easily fixes in place the idea that since 'his car has one spare seat' it means that you must take the driver seat. This happens automatically, and feels so obvious that it becomes our base-line starting point.

Lateral thinking was a term introduced by Edward De Bono to contrast with what he termed the 'vertical', formal thinking that we usually employ. While vertical thinking is top-down, lateral thinking, as its name implies, has greater breadth or span. It can jump across disciplinary lines, much as happens during brainstorming sessions at work. It is a technique for looking beyond the obvious, wonderfully dancing around constraints, but at the same time not ignoring them. The creative mind or the creative mind-state is free-associating, connecting different parts of the brain. It is, in essence, bottom-up thinking. Our brains become elastic, yielding crazy idea combinations in addition to insights. Compare with the top-down, hierarchical nature of academic thought, where the path to the solution to the problem presented above is blocked at the very outset. Here you should be able to see that vertical thinking is convergent thinking and lateral thinking is divergent thinking.

People vary in the degree to which they embrace these very different ways of thinking. But we all have the capacity for both – the brain furnishes us with cautious, careful, rational, organised ways of thinking and scattered, creative, inspired ways of thinking. They are like muscles – exercising them can improve them.

The most famous lateral thinking problem appears baffling to most people. A man walks into a bar and asks the barman for a glass of water. The barman pulls out a gun and points it at the man. The man says 'thank you' and walks out.

Why?

As soon as a gun is introduced, our minds latch onto the aggressive, life-threatening character it is imbued with. The answer to the puzzle is to see it differently. The barman had noticed that the man was hiccuping, and asked for water to try to stop it (but we had not known this crucial fact). Understanding that hiccuping can be arrested with a sudden shock, he drew the gun on the man. An unconventional but effective remedy. You see the pattern here is that we can be fact-bound. The facts have a gravity that stymies our thinking.

Another classic lateral thinking problem can hopefully make you experience this gravity. Originated I believe by Paul Wason, you are told that there is a pattern behind the number sequence :

246

You are tasked with determining the pattern. You are to give your own sequence of three numbers, to which the task setter will respond by saying if they adhere to the pattern. You can repeat this as many times as you like. At any time you can offer guesses of the pattern. Of course, many will offer a first pattern such as this :

8 10 12

The setter will confirm that this fits the pattern. So you try another :

$$27 \ 29 \ 31$$

The setter will again confirm that the pattern matches. Most people will proffer such confirming sequences. This convergent thinking approach has been drilled into them by the education system. The term sequence will couple, in their minds, with the ascending nature of 2, 4, 6 to narrow their thinking to sets of numbers in *ascending* sequence. They are blinded to the reality that these too are number sequences :

$$734$$

$$-8 \qquad 3.6 \qquad 3,000$$

The word 'sequence' has *primed* their thinking. More subtly, education conditioning has made most of us adverse to negative answers as discussed earlier. So we stay in the comfort zone of offering sequences that will likely yield a positive answer.

If we were to pause – to think – we would realise that no number of confirmation answers gets us to 100% surety of a definitive solution. Some will stretch their thinking a little with sequences such as this :

$$20 \quad 40 \quad 60$$

However, when that also yields a confirmation, they remain stuck. Instead, if they felt that the pattern was a series of evenly spaced numbers, for example, then they should offer a sequence that is not, to challenge their theory, to actively try to get a negative response :

$$2 \quad 7 \quad 20$$

And when that too receives a confirmation, they might start to think divergently and loosen their minds up – escaping the pull of gravity of preconceived ideas. So they might try a very different sequence :

$$5 \ 5 \ 5$$

And now they get a **no** answer. Their first failure to match the pattern. In spite of what school taught you, this is *good news*. They try some another pattern, encouraged by the success of a no answer :

$$6 \quad 4 \quad 2$$

That too yields a **no**. Now they are in a much better position to venture a guess as to the pattern. It is akin to a new pool player at your club – you cannot really know his strength no matter how many games he wins until you see him lose. So they ask if it is a series of positive ascending numbers? The answer is also **no**.

Still, they are trapped by a converging thinking approach. Just because they were offered a nice orderly pattern at the start, they were pulled by the gravity and comfort of that niceness, failing to see that the solution might be a more generalised pattern, of which 2, 4, 6 is a particularly neat example. Finally, they might eventually discover that the pattern is simply 'ascending numbers'.

Very, very few people get that solution. Try it on some friends. Now that you know the pitfalls you will be able to see more clearly than before how convergent thinking so readily constrains us. The gravity of knowledge and convergent thinking is more powerful than we realise. If you are able, try it with someone you know who has psychosis. They may be far more able to think divergently, their condition in effect a consequence of too much divergent thinking.

The innovator mindset

The innovative, entrepreneurial mind can often see how things could be, rather than as they are now – they *feel* shortcomings with the status quo, and the *discontent* that this engenders urges them to *explore* better ways.

James Dyson was frustrated by a decades-old design paradigm. He hated the inefficiency of traditional bagged vacuum cleaners, reasoning that there must be a better way. So he experimented endlessly to finally develop a working replacement cyclone mechanism, creating thousands of prototypes in the process. To illustrate the gravity of 'this is how things are' thinking, manufacturers like Hoover were unimpressed by his design and spurned his innovation. So he built his own factory and manufactured the cyclone cleaners himself. Having then changed the paradigm, Hoover and others followed suit.

The creative mindset

Innovation is in effect a subset of creativity, the broader sweep embracing the arts and design and even (or especially) engineering solutions. Creative thinking is essentially unbounded thinking. It is generally free-flowing, liberal and only loosely tied to the delivery of an end product or service. At least in the early 'incubation' stage. Ideas from that stage can then get fleshed out in a different kind of creative phase, where they are twisted and manipulated. In delivering a product or service, however, a more rigorous approach in the final phase is needed, bounded as it is by target or delivery constraints. But even then, it is common to step back to revisit the creative stage when it becomes clear there are persistent shortcomings in the deliverable so far.

For many, creativity is presumed to be an exclusively artistic domain. But it is, in fact, foundational to many other fields as I mentioned before. When designing the first iPhone, for instance, the designers likely had a creative insight to push for the inclusion of an orientation sensor – a more elegant way than screen buttons for determining landscape or portrait display format. When linear thinking prevails in company culture, however, the software team might likely be given no leverage on phone hardware functionality decision making. They would be obliged to generate a software solution – the user would have to press a button to change orientation rather than just rotate the device. The divisions within such a company reinforce hierarchical thinking. Creative thinking flourishes in a broader, cross-discipline, inclusive, enabling culture.

The aforementioned Albert Einstein used to take mental trips out in space to feel how light beams might propagate. He used his creativity to explore beyond known facts to help his theories lead to paradigm- shifting breakthroughs. The kind of 'day-dreaming' that school tends to frown upon. As if it is only when you show *external*, material signs of mental activity does your thinking ever count, so dominant is the quantitative mindset.

The creative, innovative mindset starts to see not how things *are* but how things *might be*. So often we look at the things around us in simple, normalised ways. We see *a flower* rather than *this flower* in all its unique glory. When we start to look beyond the habitual, practical, normalised ways that the economical brain prefers to adopt, we begin to see that things could be very different.

Beds are a foot or two above the ground. Why is that the case? Do we really need to be so close to the floor? What if we elevated the bed a few feet higher, and created a storage area underneath? What if it were so big we could walk inside?

We see the paved roads and pavements. We see countless parked cars. This is so commonplace that it becomes normalised, and we no longer really see that it is a scar on the landscape, trampling over natural land. If we *really* challenged the notion that we should have personal cars, then we might remove many of these roads, a large number of which are effectively car parks most of the time (the average car is moving about 5% of the time). Imagine the delight of pollution-free, grass covered tracts between rows of houses and shops (read further in "After the Car"). The creative mind can envisage such areas, picture what might

136

be rather than what is. A mind free to challenge convention and conventional thinking.

Prams were originally built like tiny cars. However, they were hard to move onto buses and took up rather a lot of space inside them. They were always made this way, so surely that was the right way they had to be made? Of course not, the creative mind mocking such conventional thinking. Owen Finlay Maclaren saw the problem quite clearly back in 1965. He was working on the collapsable Supermarine Spitfire undercarriage and was able to envisage the concept as transferable to the design of buggies or pushchairs. He was, fortunately, able to carry through the idea right through to patent – creativity is not so vital until we deliver on its potential.

Paintings appear in a wide range of rectangular frames or the rare oval frame. Why? The ease and repeatability of manufacture normalised these shapes and killed interest in other shapes. For the creative mind, though, they are not bound by such 'framing' conventions. Why not make a triangular frame or four linked circles that represent the seasons? Why must we have a flat canvas? Challenge what is – break free from the shackles of convention.

Why do tables in paved areas often rock, upsetting the drinks if knocked? It is because four legs do not sit well on uneven surfaces. Tables with three legs are stable, but it is dangerously too easy to tip them right over. What about designing feet on four-legged tables to have some give, cushioning them onto uneven surfaces? Has any team of designers explored that notion? Can you think of other ideas? Can you start engaging in new realms of thought?

In soccer, when a ball goes out of play at the end of the pitch, either a corner or goal-kick ensues. Strangely, perversely, when the ball goes out of play to the side, a throw-in follows. Why does a game that denies use of hands oblige us to use them to take throw-ins? The former Manchester United football manager Louis Van Gaal was known to challenge this, declaring that it would make far more sense for a free kick to be awarded instead since throw-ins often end up with the opposing team immediately reclaiming the ball. Clearly, what has been unchallenged in over a century of play is not there all along because it was the right thing to do.

While on the subject of soccer, did you ever pause to wonder why matches are played with eleven players? My firm belief is that ten outfield players were chosen as a nice round number. If I am correct, over a century of association football rests on what was in effect an arbitrary decision. I have played hundreds of casual, informal soccer matches on a local recreation field. A kind of community football, with streams of players coming and going week by week, year by year. Maybe sixty players will turn up on one occasion so that we have to split into two games of fifteen-a-side, not terribly enjoyable as each player gets only a fraction of time with the ball. Sometimes, harsh weather will see maybe just six players arrive, and embark on an intense game of three-a-side.

These games have made it quite clear to myself and others I have spoken to that around eight-a-side makes for the best game, albeit on a smaller pitch size (we use bags for posts). If association football had adopted such numbers, smaller pitches might have been needed, but the games would have been far more open and exciting with more goals scored. Football currently generally has fewer goals than most supporters would probably like. Rugby managed to entertain smaller sized games to good effect, but the more entrenched a rule, the less likely it is to change – even when most likely to have been arbitrary in the first place.

Creativity with numbers

For many, mathematics is hated and pointless. It is often seen as an abstract set of rules that must be followed to achieve an abstract outcome. Rarely is it taught with sufficient regard to the real world. The teaching additionally tends to condition the students into believing that for each problem presented to them, there must be one method to solve it and that obtaining a correct answer is the only meaningful part of the problem-solving exercise.

Yet mathematics has enormous scope for creativity. I was very fortunate to be blessed with a precise, analytical, logical mind, but also a pretty creative one. So I was able to tackle problems from many different angles. The light, dancing, innovative part of my mind worked in concert with the calculating part, offering different routes to attempt to solve problems until I found a successful one. My creative side also loved to seek the elegant solution, which curiously tends to be the nature of many mathematical problem answers. Alas, my wife struggled with mathematics, often choosing to make problems more complicated rather than less. Creativity is the fuel for more straightforward, smarter ways of doing things.

Let me offer a simple example. Consider this sum :

$$1 + 2 + 3 + 4 + 5 + 6 + 7 + 8 + 9$$

Those fearful of mathematics and those mechanically bound to rules will add the numbers up. The creative way is to start by estimating the answer – to calculate a ball-park figure as a guide to see if we are on track with our actual calculations. Were you taught that rough answers were valid at the start? Or were you taught that only calculations that lead to the holy grail of 'the correct answer' were acceptable?

Thinking creatively, you would explore the nature of the problem. You would then observe that the middle of the numbers (the median) is 5. Since there are nine numbers, a rough guess would be nine lots of 5 which comes to 45.

The next step that creative minds tend to follow is to look for patterns. Clearly, this is a linear, orderly sequence. I can see that if we add the first and last numbers – the 1 and the 9 – then we get 10. This is the same as adding the 2 and the 8, the next two numbers at start and end. You can envisage this pattern repeating all the way to the 4 and 6, with the 5 left over. Here we are discovering such patterns while looking at the salient features of the problem rather than trying to work out which problem type it is and which rule must be applied. The latter is like taking the cart before the horse – letting what we know determine what we see rather than let what we see determine how we respond.

So we have four lots of 10 which comes to 40, with the 5 added to give 45 as the answer. It exactly matches the guess, although guesses are often not that precise. We have our answer with fewer, easier additions courtesy of finding a pattern.

But why does the creative mind see such a pattern? I suggest that it is largely from a *feel* of the nature of numbers, which is certainly the case for myself. This in turn comes from a playful attitude towards them. An attitude that explores beyond the 'rules' the teacher gives us. The creative mind is not so readily bound to rules nor beholden to them. How about a game that fosters creative mathematical thinking? It is one I played when young, where the rules of mathematics only take you so far. You have to twist and manipulate these rules to play the game – you have to extend yourself with thinking.

The rules are simple. At each stage, you work with the numbers 1, 2, 3 and 4. You must use all of them at every stage. The first such stage is to use these numbers to manufacture a calculation that gives the result of 1. All of a sudden, you are the person creating a calculation. You are not receiving it ready-made to work on, but you are building it yourself. Here is one way to do this :

$$(1 \times 2) + 3 - 4$$

One of the beauties of this game is that there can be multiple methods yielding multiple solutions. We are liberated from the "one problem, one method, one solution" strait-jacket. That starts to free the rule-bound mind. Here is another solution :

$$(2 + 3) / (1 + 4)$$

As you would presume, the next stage is to use the same numbers to yield the value of 2.
This is easier :

$$4 + 2 - 3 - 1$$

We keep going through 3, 4, 5 and so on. We can get as far as 27 :

$$((4 \times 2) + 1) \times 3$$

But 28 leaves us shortchanged with the **+ – x /** operators that have gotten us this far. Can you however reflect now on how these have becomes tools of our trade – tools of the problem solving process?
It starts to feel like we have been using them to suit our *own* agenda.

To try to furnish a solution for 28, we can introduce the '!' factorial symbol, to add greater richness to the toolset. As a reminder :

$$2! = 2 \times 1 = \mathbf{2}$$
$$3! = 3 \times 2 \times 1 = \mathbf{6}$$
$$4! = 4 \times 3 \times 2 \times 1 = \mathbf{24}$$

And for good measure, we can also add powers to our toolset, such as **3** raised to the power of **2** giving us **9**.

All being well, these new tools will animate problem solvers further. They will embrace something that helps them. These operators start to feel like real-world devices rather than abstractions, even though the problem set itself is essentially abstract. The tools of mathematics are being used in earnest.

So we can calculate 28 now using the factorial operator, for example:

$$4! + 3 + 2 - 1$$

How far can you reach with this series? Would you need to introduce more tools to go further? What tools could you find?

Pain
The counterintuitive nature of pain

Living creatures survive by adapting. The well-endowed brain that humans have gives our species a huge adaptation advantage over all others. We even modify the environment to adapt to us rather than vice versa.

Adaptation requires foresight in addition to flexible reactivity to changing circumstances. In both cases, the brain predicts what might be happening around us from past or current clues. The sound of soft footsteps might have signalled to our ancestors the approach of a wild animal stalking them. Historically, we evolved to predict the worst, just in case.

Even the simple act of moving our hand to pick up a mug of tea is a largely predictive process. The traffic of signals to the muscles to make the movement is not uni-directional. The feedback that the brain is interested in from the proprioception (the sense of movement) signals from our arm is only where it differs from what is predicted. The brain is interested in novelty – such as if our fingers slipped when grabbing the mug handle.

The prediction of a dangerous animal approaching acts to protect us from potential fatal harm. Such circumstances are fortunately rare these days. More common than fatal feline strikes is a sports or running injury, where the brain seeks to protect us from aggravation of that injury. So it creates pain.

It also predicts that harm might arise if tissue such as muscle is activated near the site of the injury. So a thigh strain will cause the brain to create pain when any part of the affected leg is moved.

The pain will appear to emanate from the injury site, but that is a clever trick by the brain. The pain is created in the brain and experienced in the mind – it is projected onto the injury site.

The established consensus until recent revelations in neuroscience was that the level and nature of pain was proportional to the degree and nature of injury. But the correlation has been found to be poor.

It has been discovered that pain is solely a predictive and protective mechanism. The brain calculates what pain level is needed to make us protect the injury site. Extraordinary in this calculation is that it considers your history (such as past injuries), your nature (such as emotional and physical sensitivity), the environment (if you are escaping from a dangerous situation, the pain signal will actually be deferred), and the damage signals from the site.

Pain level is therefore a calculation of protection needed, not a measure of damage status. This is a profound matter, as you will see shortly.

Each day that the pain signal is created to protect the damaged site, the brain gets better at creating it. So much so that it appears to get lazy. It can trigger pain without consultation with the site. It seems to stop tracking the healing process.

Even when an injury or infection heals, the brain can continue to trigger pain when the former injury site is mobilised. This is especially likely in Neurotic character types where the mind is often obsessively protective because pain is felt more intensely.

Frozen shoulder appears to fall into the category of pain sustained after healing completes. Pain has become a false signal through sheer neural habit – what neural pathways are exercised most often become more likely to trigger. So our simple emotional reaction to mobilising of the area that keeps giving us pain will trigger that network into creating the pain again. A vicious negative feedback loop.

Since the brain is clearly at fault – there is no longer a functional, physiological problem that needs protecting with pain – we must use psychology to remedy the false pain scenario. This is, of course, easier said than done, and Health systems around the world are still playing catch-up with this reality.

A very important problem here is knowing how to identify when healing has actually completed. Clearly, we cannot be sure that pain is a reliable guide! Instead, the anticipated healing time for the nature of injury is used as a guide. When healing is likely to have finished, we should be mobilising the site *in defiance of, or disregard to* the pain level. We focus on the movement and not the pain.

Here, we are easing away neural pathways that are falsely stuck in a protection state. We replace them with new *things are alright but my brain is giving false pain signals* neural pathways.

There are factors, however, that actually serve to increase the level and duration of pain, regardless of site healing progress.

If we focus on pain rather than envisage healing and keep mobilising the body, then we make it a bigger, entrenched issue.

If we fear the pain, the same happens.

If we have low self-esteem or are depressed, the pain will increase, and likely feedback to make us feel emotionally even worse creating a chronic downward cycle of behaviour.

If we feel that we are a *victim* – that we should be healing by now, or 'why am I so unlucky?' – the body will respond accordingly and play out the injury longer.

Pain may be sensed as physical, but it is very much a matter of mind.

What follows now in this chapter is distillation of the best book on resolving the problem that you are likely to read. "Unlearn your pain" by Howard Schubiner and Michael Betzold. The 2023 version I have been reading is the 4th edition, with the most supremely clear and empathic writing it would seem humanly possible to create, backed by decades of scientific research findings.

For some reason that is not entirely clear in the books I have read on the subject, pain is created as a protection mechanism for psychological/mental ailments such as social anxiety. My own view on this is that the brain does not create pain as defence. For social anxiety for example, it can tense us up to make us more alert to how the 'awkward' social scenario is panning out. It is that tensing repeated often enough that can become a tension headache. Once that happens, the defensive tensing action more likely triggers a headache. We are caught on a slippery negative feedback slope.

With both physical and psychological pain, that pain symptom is a false flag, no matter how painful. There is no physical problem.

Nerve data from the site of an injury or an infection is only the first part of the pain creation process. It tends to determine the nature of the pain, such as burning, tingling or intense sensory feelings. But accompanying these are two other dimensions. Emotions and thinking accompany the pain. We might worry, fear, or even become frustrated by the pain. And we will also try to understand the problem creating the pain, projecting ahead and maybe catastrophising that it will never heal.

The level and nature of the pain is there to protect against further damage. But the brain takes the emotional and thinking factors into its calculated level and nature of pain. And our history and nature. After enough time passes, the correlation between pain level and site healing is poor because the pain level and nature is determined by these factors more than the site signals. Pain is therefore described now as a *biopsychosocial* phenomenon.

In nervous, sensitive or neurotic people, the pain level can be high *and* this can feedback negatively into the emotional and thinking reactions to this pain. You can become trapped in a vicious feedback loop. The pain becomes so dominant in the mind and feelings that it has a gravity of attention that reinforces the perceived need for that pain. What is attended to often grows.

The result is a set of neural networks in the brain that create the brain ever more readily. Compounding this are associations that are created that add to the emotional and thinking negative feedback forces – when stressed, pain level rises and the scenario causing the stress now becomes a new trigger for pain upscaling, even if it does not cause stress the next time.

When pain persists after healing completes – when there is no longer a functional pathology that should be soliciting that pain – the pain is described as a *Mind Body Syndrome (MBS)*. The most likely people to suffer MBS are sensitive caring people – good people. Those who are very conscientious, put great demands on themselves and care greatly about their impact on others. A sad paradox.

Conditions such as tension headaches, migraine, fybromyalgia, back pain are often MBS pains. Even tingling legs can be fabrications of the mind no longer caused by a real physical problem.

I will pay respect to the "Unlearn your pain" book by only briefly covering the therapy techniques used to resolve MBS.

Key is to accept that no matter the pain level, MBS pain has no physical cause – it is 'simply' a neural network stuck in habit triggering. It overreacts to trigger causes, of which there can be many. We must focus on the retraining of these trigger reactions to revert the brain to the normal responses that now lay dormant. Then the pain path will fade into oblivion.

While we do this, we must avoid the desire to track progress, or be impatient, or get upset that some of the reconditioning solicits greater pain. We must, counter-intuitively, adopt an indifferent attitude to the pain. And, also counter-intuitively, be indifferent to progress. We must detach from expectation and progress and focus solely on the retraining. Attend to the execution rather than the outcome of our efforts.

And to relax into this process by not fussing how long it takes. Do not be hard on yourself!

The retraining is in two parts – learning relaxation and meditation to calm our immune system down – and to address each trigger we identify as increasing or sustaining our pain. Often, the pain has made us avoid increasing more parts of life. We may stop meeting in large groups if that triggers panic attacks, for example. Instead, we should acclimatise ourselves to these situations. We must embrace to one degree or other, the very things in life causing us pain!

All while not fussing about whether the pain rises or falls as a consequence. We just keep chipping away.

Today, for example, I encountered a more elderly lady that I occasionally see near my road. I normally try to keep the chat brief as she can rant for ages. Today I let her rant. Just observed her face – even though not so pleasant to look at – and did so without judgement or alarm. And sustained attention with occasional but salient interrupts to try to call short the stream of words. Maybe this went on for 3 to 5 minutes. But the feeling of empowerment embracing what I normally avoid made the whole encounter a calm matter. No obvious pain elevation resulted (and yes, a casual observation of pain levels is OK).

There may be many triggers, some you are not really aware of. Mindfulness as a general part of your life can really help you observe early the start of a trigger.

If you have had pain a long time, the reversal may take weeks, months of even years. But it can also often proceed rapidly. You can experience a positive feedback loop where the process starts working and you relax into it, thereby making further change more likely.

I wish you well! Let me know if you succeed dealing with a chronic problem that seemed intractable.

Talking with strangers

A vital habit that is sadly dying away

Here in Britain, we tend to teach our children not to talk to strangers. It aligns with the British culture, which also asks us to speak only when spoken to first. Quite how that is supposed to work, who knows. Maybe that is why we often struggle to talk with strangers beyond a simple 'hello, how are you?'. And then we often forget to tell children when they grow up that it is now OK to talk to strangers.

Part of the problem is that we use a judgemental word to describe people we do not know. They are, somehow, *strange*. We do not mean that when we refer to strangers, but the implication still permeates the meaning. Better to see that they are *new, unknown* people rather than strange. And maybe also *knowable* by implication. The words we choose carry much greater weight than we often realise.

Besides, even when growing up, every person we meet is essentially a stranger the very first time we encounter them, even if a family member. And it may well be the case that some aunts, uncles and grandparents are harder for children to relate to than the other children they meet and play with in parks or in school.

Historically, fear of strangers has deep roots in our genetic past. Close-knit tribal communities tended to treat those of other tribes with hostility. A stranger was someone generally to be feared (or mated with). Unlike most animals, however, humans have evolved to intermingle with strangers on a daily basis in towns and cities. We generally underestimate how much of an achievement this has been, vital as it is to the fluid functioning of urban life. Alcohol can readily undo this social arrangement, so it is still a bit delicate.

In the US and increasingly in Britain, a darwinian 'survival of the fittest' individualism is being promoted by governments. This can and does undermine the social fabric and can regress us to hold more primitive fears of strangers. Or simply a fear of 'others'.

Yet business thrives on the synergy of people working for a common good. The many are greater than the sum of their number. In society also, where the meeting places such as coffee shops, pubs, theatre and shopping centres act as social lubricants. They connect people and enhance those connections. But they do so much more readily when we are receptive to others. When we are prepared to talk with strangers. When we put our own agenda behind that of others. Where we show genuine interest in the unknown, but knowable life of each person we might choose to talk to the first time.

Sometimes, it is no more than a few exchanged words.

Sometimes, it can lead to a sustained conversation.

Sometimes it can lead to a friendship.

The more that we explore and embrace connections with others, the more we enter the web of human relations. The atoms we are composed of are themselves parts of great webs – likewise the cells in our body. Underlying themes of the Universe are connectivity and interaction. It is a kind of calling, where the absence of such is isolation that can see us atrophy and fade away, denied meaning from others in effect.

And if you think that talking with strangers is a matter for extrovert, bullish, outward going people, then you are wrong! It may take time for shy and introverted types to connect with others, but repeated, simple hellos and brief exchanges will reveal the reality that most people most of the time are nice and are happy to talk about themselves. So a fear of talking with strangers is often unfounded.

Anatomy of an epidemic

I often carry two or three books with me in my capacious backpack, but the past few days only one, so good is it. "Anatomy of an epidemic" is a fairly long, but cleverly well organised and researched exposure of flaws in the treatment of mental health conditions in the US.

By way of example, it explains that anti-psychotic drugs do not work as they should. They seek to decrease a presumed excess of dopamine. The brain reacts to the reduction by increasing dopamine receptor sensitivity. It seeks to fix the imbalance the drug is trying to create! When the patient stops taking the drug, normal dopamine levels resume and the increased sensitivity of receptors creates a worse problem than they had in the first place. At least this is how I have understood the central theme of the book.

Before taking my seat in Waterloo tea shop to read, I spoke to a very friendly lady, **Laura**, from Northern Ireland. A viola player by profession, happy to read a draft copy of this book. On my way home, I crossed paths with **Boyd Clack**. This time, I asked him what he was up to – was he working. He was happy to talk about a film he has a small part in. It is all about the actress **Carol Hawkins** and her fight with *schizophrenia!* So I was naturally well positioned to talk about this subject.

Boyd raised a key point that the book has yet to cover, but which is of course absolutely vital to this debilitating mental health condition – if existing drugs are abandoned because of long term effects, what do you use in place of them? For many people, the short term benefits are so immense that long term effects have to be tolerated. I hope this subject matter is not too sad or tedious. But if mental health issues are alien to you, be grateful – be very grateful as they can create a deep, deep spiral. One aspect that **Boyd** talked of most fiercely was that chronic depression for him was at root so *extremely boring*. Vast amounts of time spent in a lack-lustre, lifeless mental state that is by definition devoid of excitement, rhythm – of anything – that can stir the soul.

Abergavenny food festival

Every September, Abergavenny hosts a large food festival. Not all are blessed with blue sky and 24C heat. So I emboldened myself for a near two hour bus journey and resumed my scenery gazing hobby.

It was in Cwmbran, I believe, that a lady a little older than I boarded and sat next to me. She was an easy talker and good listener, and we embarked on a thirty minute chat. At one point, I declared that I was really enjoying the chat but as an introvert was equally getting tired. It was a sign of her ease with me that I could say that. She also said the same, and we were, briefly as if one person. Quite a comforting feeling.

It transpires that **Mair De-Gare Pitt**, for that is her unusual name, is a published writer. Mostly poetry. She teaches also, and when seeking an artist to illustrate a recent book discovered that one of her students was more than capable for the task. Surprisingly, some of her former oil paintings matched some of the poems ludicrously well. I necessarily mentioned that I was also a writer and that I was writing this book. I regaled the most recent story involving **Boyd Clack** only to discover that she knows him as he had attended one of her poetry sessions. Quite the small, connected world it seems.

Survival of the fittest?

The American dream promotes individual success – that you will be supported in your endeavours to work hard and succeed. It largely rests upon the literal US adoption of Charles Darwin's concept of the *survival of the fittest*.

Two caveats

There are two problems with this predication, the first trivial, the second somewhat not.

It was actually the philosopher Herbert Spencer who coined that phrase. However, it did not sit well with Darwin's philosophy of life, so he only used the phrase reluctantly some time after first publication of his famous book on evolution "On the origin of species".

But the concept of the *survival of the fittest* necessarily encapsulates only a narrow view of life and evolution, not least because life is about reproduction and relationships as well as survival. And what is the subject of this phrase – an individual or a species?

You will also see that *fitness* is only one category that affects survival and reproduction of a species.

Survival of the fittest is not a natural thing either :

> *When cells in our bodies turn rogue, for instance, the result is cancer. So elaborate mechanisms have evolved to maintain cooperation and suppress selfishness, such as cellular "surveillance" programmes that trigger cell suicide if they start to turn cancerous.*
>
> *Looked at from this point of view, the concept of the survival of the fittest could be used to justify socialism rather than laissez-faire capitalism. Then again, the success of social insects could be used to argue for totalitarianism. Which illustrates another point: it is nonsense to appeal to the "survival of the fittest" to justify any economic or political ideology, especially on the basis that it is "natural".*

Another matter

There is a more subtle misconception we should address first. That each living thing now is *optimally* developed to suit its environment, tuned by centuries of evolutionary adaptations. The reality is that all living things are a work in progress, constantly evolving, but not necessarily adapting. Adaption is a longer time process – at any one time, we living things can be a mix of appropriate and inappropriate natures and bodies for the environment we find ourselves in. We may find that we have yet to adapt to big city life for example. We may suffer mental malaises as a result of the stresses in trying to do so. And we have yet to fully adapt beyond earlier, more pastoral times, that characterised the bulk of our existence.

We are social creatures

Humans are a pretty unique species by virtue of the degree to which we cooperate. We are fundamentally *social* creatures, becoming so in order to reap the benefits of the synergy of group life and to support the advantages of monogynous child-rearing.

Humans have evolved to be socially minded. We rely on the social transmission of knowledge and culture, avoiding the need for each young person to learn life skills by slow personal discovery and trial and error. The other primates remain stuck at low developmental levels because they have not developed this transmission phase.

Social success and harmony relies on a compromise of selfish needs to suit group needs.

We *do* compete, but within group frameworks. We compete with *support* from others. Few businesses can run with no employees.

The ability to behave altruistically is a part of our social inheritance. We may lay our life down for our children, even if we are *fitter* at what we do than they will ever be.

Luck

Luck has an enormous part to play in both survival and reproduction of individuals and of a species. You might just happen to meet the right person at the right time and have children that prosper. Or you might get into the wrong relationship by pure bad luck. You might fall irreversibly in love with someone who is infertile.

Did you ever notice how many children's picture books are written by celebrities? It is not that they are *necessarily* the fittest to write such books, but that they are likely to yield better sales because of the weight that their fame brings to the books.

After forest fires have extinguished themselves, a surprisingly common and natural matter, the seeds that germinate and grow are those that happen to land on the fertile land left behind. Survival by virtue of being in the right place at the right time. Luck more than anything else.

Status

How often, I wonder, have students puzzled as to why an incoherent professor at the front of a lecture theatre ever got to lecture them. Was he really chosen because of his ability to lecture?

In most cases, no. Professors lecture as a consequence of their status and position. To teach is a very different skill, however, than to flourish through a Masters and PhD. Again, the fittest is not necessarily the most capable.

By the same token, ex-footballers tend to sail through their coaching certificates by virtue of their ability with a football, not as a result of natural skill in coaching other footballers (although there are some notable exceptions to this). Some of the best coaches never reached a high level playing the game.

Microsoft Windows was often weaker in functionality and performance than Apple Operating Systems, but always grabbed a larger market share. Marketing created a status for Windows that made them a preferential purchase in spite of a relative inferiority.

And finally

So what can we conclude from these thoughts?

Maybe we should look beyond qualifications when finding the best person?

Maybe we can give more credit for work produced by 'unknown' people – new actors, artists and authors can get their chance when currently denied no matter how good they are?

Maybe political systems that promote individual success at the expense of social cohesion and welfare may danger the very social, cooperative nature of humans that separates us from animals, thereby compromising life for everyone, at least to a degree?

Maybe we can strive to see humans of different ethnicities, or religious persuasions as people we can cooperate rather than compete with?

There is an interesting concept I recently discovered, where humans often evolve to be 'tamer' much as wild dogs and cats are tamed to be social companions for humans. Our own taming is to make us cohere better in groups.

This moves us to a position where *survival of the group* is more appropriate, the individual needs supplied via group membership.

Work

Our preconceptions about work

At the basic level, work is the expenditure of energy.

In everyday terms, work is an activity done for someone for payment.

But this is a *conditioned* definition we have been conditioned to accept. We have, in effect, been indoctrinated into seeing work in a narrow sense.

You see how there are two deviations from the basic level definition of work :

- That the work must be for someone else

- That it must be paid for

We are so heavily conditioned to see work in this way that it blinds us to many of the real values humans can offer to the World. One of the very basic examples is that of a 'Housewife', a demeaning term for a fundamentally crucial role. Because there is no direct payment for the service of bringing up children, caring for the home, shopping, and preparing meals, we treat it with far too little respect. It is not seen as 'work' nor as a 'job'.

There are more subtle examples. I have personally been preoccupied with guilt on too many occasions when I take my daily or twice daily trips to coffee shops. I do recognise how very lucky I am to be able do this. That I might be seen as *merely lazing around*, and *obviously not working* is also a reflection of our conditioning of the meaning of work. I often study non-fiction books with my coffee, so I am in effect actually working. But there again, because I am not on a formal educational course, this also does not count! That I can read and absorb and develop ideas from what I read does not grant it the status of 'working' because *the system* disqualifies it.

Here is another example.

A friend I have acquired via these cafe visits has been struggling with his life lately. I have chatted with him, giving him emotional support, and guidance gleaned from some of the many books I have read. He was sufficiently grateful to hug me. Twice.

Yet to a bystander, we were just idling time away. At best, I was being a good friend. But no way was I deemed to be 'working'. Yet in a very real sense, I was. I was expended energy to help him. I was working for his benefit. Because, however, I was not qualified, employed, or paid to be a counsellor, then what I was doing was not 'work' in our acquired sense.

So I was 'not' working only because of arbitrary labels. If I did the very same things as a counsellor, I would have been deemed to be working.

More subtly, I was applying knowledge hard earned from my book studies. So when you see me reading in a coffee shop, rather than see me as 'just' relaxing, it may be more prudent to see me as both relaxing and researching – extending myself for the benefit of both myself and others.

The process of seeing work in a more generalise sense is very similar indeed to the journey I went through to liberate myself from religious indoctrination to become an atheist, albeit one who tries to respect religious people.

It is only in the process of addressing the indoctrination that you first become aware of it. This itself is an enlightening exercise.

When you think about people toiling away at work, just realise that the capitalist mechanism, underpinned in many ways by competition, results in many people duplicating in large part what their competitors do. This is fundamentally wasteful – many companies have their own suite of extremely expensive computer systems, for example, that do pretty well much what their rival company systems do. There are now far too many product varieties on the shelves of our shops than we need as a result of competition – research shows that we prefer less choice.

Imagine what we could do without that duplication of effort?

Imagine how things would change if work was more intelligently defined?

Some of my drawings

From a photo of the Queen mother aged 7

Judy Garland from a photo

Julianne Michelle US actor aged 7, from a photo

I was born in London, now living in Cardiff, the capital of Wales. A former BBC Engineer and IBM Programmer, I have a mixed background, including years of cabinet making, photography, drawing, painting, writing ... and lots of talking.

The notion behind this book is to share matters that have been emotionally compelling to me. The Oriental game of Go, for example, has been a wonderful escape from the tensions as well as a perfect means of expressing the twin axioms of left and right brain thinking.

Balancing Act is a moralistic short novel that I felt compelled to write as a means of expressing key atheist and religious feelings and thoughts.

The essays express strong opinions about how things are and how they might be different. I inherited from my father a way of seeing not what is but what could be in ways that seem to strangely pass most people by. This is not an arrogant matter – I repeat that I inherited this faculty rather than being its creator. All I can do and have done is to cultivate it as a means of gratitude.

Printed in Great Britain
by Amazon